World Book of Interesting **FACTS**

World Book
of Interesting **FACTS**

by The Editors of **The World Book Encyclopedia**

Published by

World Book–Childcraft International, Inc.
A subsidiary of The Scott & Fetzer Company

Chicago London Paris Sydney Tokyo Toronto

Contents

Introduction:
An eye to facts

Facts are known to be true. Facts are known to have happened. And facts—the details of life—are a real challenge to learn.

Why is this so? One reason is that learning details is a difficult task. Remembering them may be harder still. Also, details are not always presented in an interesting way. Have you ever tried to read a list of figures or names for pleasure? Chances are you did not keep with it for very long.

But did you know that learning facts can actually be fun? The *World Book of Interesting FACTS*, prepared by the editors of *The World Book Encyclopedia*, is designed to take the threat out of learning details. *FACTS* is a well-organized and thoroughly researched volume. It presents a large number of details in an interesting way: through conversation and illustration.

Would you like to know why the sky looks blue? You'll find that question and its answer in this book of facts. Do you believe in walking fish? You will after you read the *FACTS* chapter on fascinating animals.

In the easy dialog of these informal chapters, there are many topics other than the heavens and the animals. *FACTS* talks about the arts, sports, and famous people. It teaches about modern technology and modern nations. It explores the world of plants and the structure of human beings.

An accurate and up-to-date sampling from all these subjects and more is available in *FACTS*. Selected illustrations from all topics make information pop out at you in a way that will help you remember what you have learned.

The information here can be used as a springboard into many activities. First, of course, the chapters themselves make for entertaining reading. In addition, they introduce interesting topics for further research.

Develop parts of these chapters into reports—even lessons. The 16-page index will help you find any other information in the book relating to your chosen topic. Finally, the question-and-answer format and conversational style of the chapters easily lend them to oral presentation.

Facts—how many are there? Certainly too many for any one person to know or for any one book to present. But interesting ones? That's a different matter. You'll find many of them in the *World Book of Interesting FACTS*.

THE EDITORS

Exploring the universe

What is the universe?

It's all the matter, light, and other forms of radiation
and energy that humankind has discovered. The
universe also is said to consist of everything that man
believes to be present somewhere in space and time
as a result of his theories.

But what is the universe specifically?

The earth and everything on it and around it, the sun
and the other planets, and all the stars. Plus clouds of
dust and gas.

How many stars are there?

There are so many that they are practically uncounta-
ble, but we could say at least 200 billion billion stars.

Stars, however, are clustered together in a form we call a galaxy, and there are millions, perhaps billions, of galaxies scattered through space.

What is a galaxy?

It's a system of stars, dust, and gas—all held together by gravity. Large galaxies have more than a trillion stars, and small galaxies fewer than a billion.

Do we live in a galaxy?

Yes, we do. It's called the Milky Way and it's huge. In fact, it is so big that light, which travels 186,282 miles (299,792 kilometers) per second, takes about 100,000 years to travel from one end to the other. Our solar system is a tiny speck located about 30,000 light-years from the center of the galaxy.

How come we don't measure by miles instead of light-years?

Because the distances in the universe between and among the galaxies are so great, it might take half a page to give them in miles. So, we measure by light-years: the distance that light travels in a year, which is about 5,880,000,000,000 miles (9,460,000,000,000 kilometers).

Can we see any galaxies besides our own without a telescope?

Yes, three. In the Northern Hemisphere we can see Andromeda Nebula, more than 2 million light-years away. In the Southern Hemisphere, we find the Small and Large Magellanic Clouds, about 200,000 light-years away.

How can we see these far-distant stars with our naked eye? Are stars so big?

The largest star is about a thousand times larger than the sun. The smallest is only about 10 miles (16 kilometers) in diameter.

Does space have an end?

Astronomers do not know if the universe has a certain size, but most of them think that bright, unusual galaxies called *quasars* may be the most distant objects in the universe. Quasars may be as far away as 10 billion light-years from earth, and moving farther away.

Quasars moving farther away? Wouldn't that make the universe bigger?

Scientists think so. They believe, by observing the *red shift* (the apparent change in the wave lengths of light from quasars), that the quasars *are* moving farther away from us and each other. The universe seems to be expanding.

Are there some things in the universe that contract?

Yes, there are what the astronomers call *black holes* because they are invisible. Recently, astronomers observed a star that orbited what seemed to be an invisible object in the constellation Cygnus. Since they assumed that a star in orbit had to orbit around something, they guessed that it was a large star that had collapsed inwardly from its own weight. They reasoned that the extreme density of the collapsed star caused its surface gravitational force to increase tremendously so that light cannot escape. The black hole, then, is invisible. But the "hole" may attract and retain nearby orbiting objects, including comets and planets.

Are there many black holes?

Yes, if you go along with one group of astronomers. They believe that black holes make up as much as a third of the material in the earth's galaxy, the Milky Way.

Just what is a star?

A huge ball of glowing gas in the sky. The two main gases making up a star are hydrogen and helium. If the star runs out of hydrogen, it may then explode into a huge cloud of gas and dust.

What makes stars shine?

Deep within the star, hydrogen gas changes into helium gas through a process called nuclear fusion. During this process, the amount of helium produced does not equal the amount of hydrogen used up. Some of the material that makes up the original hydrogen changes into energy rather than into helium. This energy that is produced passes into space as light, heat, and radio waves.

How long does a star go on shining?

Stars shine until they use up all their hydrogen. Astronomers believe that most stars have enough hydrogen to last billions of years.

Why can't we see the stars during the day?

Because sunlight brightens the sky too much for the stars to be seen.

What is the largest object in our solar system?

The sun is the largest object in our solar system. If the sun were the size of the Sears Tower (1,454 feet; 443 meters), the earth would be the size of a person standing next to it. The moon would be the size of a cocker spaniel standing next to the person.

Is that why the sky is blue?

When you look at the sky, you look up through a
layer of air that surrounds the earth. As sunlight shines
through this layer of air, it strikes tiny particles of gas
called molecules. The molecules scatter sunlight in all
directions. They scatter blue light more than other
kinds so the sky looks blue.

How do the stars move?

The stars—including our sun—only seem to "move"
across the sky. This "movement" really comes from
the spinning of the earth, not from the movement of
the stars.

Then the stars don't move after all?

Yes, they do move. But since they are so far away
from us, we can't see their actual movements. The
sun itself moves at a speed of 12 miles (19 kilometers)
per second through the Milky Way. In addition, the
sun and all the stars of the Milky Way sweep around
the center of the galaxy. This spinning motion of the
galaxy gives the sun and the stars near it a speed of
156 miles (250 kilometers) per second.

If the stars "move," how do sailors use them to navigate?

To find a ship's position, a sailor picks three stars and
measures the angle that each makes with the horizon.
He uses an almanac to find the earthly position
associated with each of the stars at the time its angle
was measured. He then calculates the distance of his
ship from each of the three positions. His ship's
location is the place on the map where the three
distance lines meet.

What are the constellations?

When ancient observers looked at the stars and began to see patterns in their arrangement, they named these patterns and mapped the stars in the year-round skies. Ursa Major (Great Bear) and Ursa Minor (Little Bear) were especially important constellations because Ursa Minor contains the North Star: an ancient guide for travelers and sailors. But, of course, the method would be imprecise compared to modern ones.

Why do ancient sailors and present-day poets call the stars "jewels of the sky"?

Because of sparkle and color. The star Rigel sparkles with a blue light; Vega appears white. Capella looks yellow, and Betelgeuse glows red.

Why do stars have different colors?

The temperature of the star's surface determines the color. Reddish stars have temperatures around 5000° F (2800° C); bluish stars 50,000° F (28,000° C). Stars of other colors have temperatures in between. Our sun, a yellowish star, has a temperature of about 10,000° F (5500° C).

Are the brighter stars the ones nearer the earth?

No, and the brighter stars aren't necessarily the bigger ones, either. Brightness also depends on the amount of light energy a star sends out. Compare the stars Rigel and Betelgeuse. Rigel is smaller and farther away from Earth, but it sends out more light energy than Betelgeuse. It is, therefore, brighter to our eye than Betelgeuse.

What else does a star send out?

A star sends out radio waves and X rays, plus other radiations that astronomers have not yet completely explained. Quasars and pulsars—celestial sources of pulsating radio waves—are in this mystery group.

I've heard that stars explode. Is that true?

Yes. One type, called a nova, becomes thousands of times brighter than normal as it explodes. Then it gradually returns to its dim appearance.

How about other types?

There is the supernova, for one, the most famous of which exploded in the Milky Way in 1054. That supernova produced such a huge cloud of dust and gas that it was given a name: the Crab Nebula.

What are the other types of stars besides the nova and supernova?

There are new ones, old ones; exploded and imploded ones—those that burst inwardly. And there are those that shine brightly and those that shine dimly.

What else do stars do?

Some of them act as double stars, or *binaries*, moving around each other. In an *eclipsing binary*, one star periodically blocks the other's light, reducing the total brightness of the two stars as seen from Earth. There are two mystery stars, too.

Mystery stars?

Astronomers call pulsars mystery stars because they

"beep," sending out a pulse of radio waves every second or so. Pulsars may be neutron stars, or stars composed not of atoms but of neutrons.

How long have we known about X rays from the stars?

Only since scientists have been able to send special telescopes above the atmosphere in rockets. The Crab Nebula sends out X rays as well as radio waves, but astronomers are not sure why.

How long do stars last?

As soon as a star begins to shine, it starts to change slowly according to its mass and the nuclear energy-producing process inside it. The life of most stars lasts billions of years, with smaller stars like our own sun taking hundreds of billions of years to change.

Why do stars change?

The supply of hydrogen decreases. Gravity overcomes pressure in the core, and the star shrinks. Then its pressure and temperature increase. During this stage, it could explode into a nova. Or it could become a white dwarf, perhaps the last visible stage of a star.

What is a white dwarf?

A star with its matter so tightly packed that the star's size might be the same as the earth's, or smaller—an unusual size for a star. A spoonful of a white star's gases would weigh tons if it could be weighed on earth. It can contract further and become either a neutron star, or the collapsed star we talked about earlier: the black hole.

What else can't we see out there between the stars besides the black holes?

Interstellar space consists of cosmic rays like protons and some atomic nuclei, as well as hydrogen, helium, and other gases.

What kind of star is the sun?

It is one of the younger generation stars astronomers call Population I. These stars were formed from gas that had been part of earlier stars.

What about distances between stars in the Milky Way?

The sun belongs to a part of the Milky Way where the distance between stars averages 4 to 5 light-years. In some other parts of the Milky Way, the stars are much closer. In globular clusters, for example, less than one-hundredth of a light-year separates the stars. As we saw before, however, the Milky Way galaxy in total is so big that it takes light 100,000 years to travel from one end to the other.

What is the star nearest the sun?

Proxima Centauri. It is 4.3 light-years away.

Why does the sun look different to us than other stars do?

Because it is the only star close enough to earth to be seen as the huge ball of glowing gas that stars are.

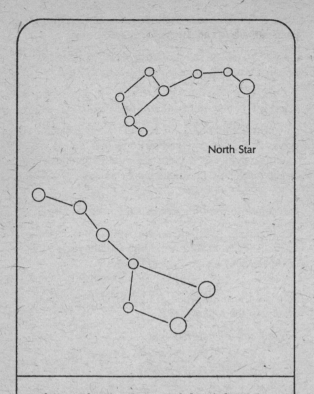

North Star

What are the Big Dipper and the Little Dipper?

These are two groups of stars seen in the northern sky. Both form the outlines of long-handled cups. The cups' positions differ depending on the time of year. On winter evenings, the Big Dipper is to the left of the Little Dipper and has its handle pointed up. The Little Dipper's handle points down. In summer, the position reverses. By early morning, the position changes again because of Earth's rotation.

What holds the sun and all the other stars in the pattern that we call the Milky Way?

Gravity. All of the stars rotate around the center, much as our nine planets rotate about the sun.

What is at the center of the Milky Way?

Scientists don't know exactly, but by studying radio waves and infrared rays, they know that there is intense activity there. Gas streams out from the center at 100 miles (160 kilometers) per second.

How close to the Milky Way is the nearest galaxy?

You might say pretty close: 200,000 light-years away. The most distant stars are billions of light-years away from the Milky Way.

So when the sun formed, it took its place revolving around in the Milky Way?

Yes, but not unaccompanied.

What is the solar system?

Well, it's the earth and the other planets, all revolving around our sun. There are various theories as to the birth of our solar system. But most scientists believe that when the sun formed more than 4.5 billion years ago from its disk of hot, swirling gases, dense regions on its edges spun off and condensed as planets, moons, and asteroids.

What are these called?

Going outward from the sun, the planets are Mercury, Venus, Earth, Mars, Jupiter, Saturn, Uranus, Neptune,

and Pluto. The sun, the planets, and their satellites—
or moons—and smaller objects called asteroids, me-
teors, and comets also make up the solar system. Add
to those, finally, interplanetary dust and interplanetary plasma.

What's the difference, then, between planets and stars?

The sun and the stars are giant, shining balls of hot
gases. The planets are dark, solid bodies, for the most
part smaller than the sun and stars. The main difference between the stars and the planets is that only the
stars produce their own heat and light.

How do you tell the difference, when looking at the sky, between a planet and a star?

They do look much alike, but you can tell them apart
in two ways. First, the planets shine with a steady
light, but the stars seem to twinkle. Second, the
planets change their positions in relation to the stars.

If planets do not produce light, how can we see them?

They reflect the light of the sun. Six of the planets—
Mercury, Venus, Mars, Jupiter, Saturn, and Uranus—
are bright enough for us to see them from the
earth without a telescope.

How hot is the sun?

The chromosphere, the reddish layer above the sun's
surface, can reach temperatures of 50,000° F (27,800°
C). The photosphere, the sun's surface, has an average temperature of 10,000° F (5500° C). The interior of
the sun is a violent furnace.

How about sizes of the planets?

According to the theory that the planets broke off from the sun during the sun's formation, they would have to be smaller than the sun. All of the planets together weigh less than a hundredth as much as the sun. The diameter of Jupiter, the largest planet, is about a tenth of the sun's diameter, and 11 times greater than Earth's. Jupiter is almost 30 times as large as Mercury, the smallest planet. Pluto's size is not known because the planet is so far from the earth (2,700,000,000 miles; 4,345,000,000 kilometers) at its shortest distance.

Are there any planets farther away than Pluto?

Astronomers do not think there are any planets in the solar system beyond Pluto. But they are almost certain that most of the stars in the universe have planets traveling around them.

Is it true that there is life on other planets?

There is no way for us to know the answer to that question yet, but we can guess at it. If we agree that there are over 100 billion galaxies, suppose one star in every galaxy had a planet like the earth, and intelligent life existed on one of every million of these planets. There would be a hundred thousand planets with intelligent life. If there are any out there, perhaps some day we will find one of them. Wouldn't that be interesting!

A look at Earth

How big is the earth?

Most people think of the earth as a huge object, and
its actual size is hard to comprehend. It weighs about
6.6 sextillion short tons (6 sextillion metric tons). Its
circumference at the equator is about 24,902 miles
(40,075 kilometers). It might help to imagine driving
between New York and San Francisco. You'd have to
make the trip more than nine times to cover the same
distance as one trip around the earth.

Isn't the earth's circumference the same no matter
where it's measured?

No. The circumference around the North and South
poles is slightly shorter than the circumference around
the equator.

Why is the polar circumference shorter?

Because the earth isn't perfectly round. It's slightly flattened at each pole and has a bulge just below the equator. It actually looks somewhat pear shaped.

How much of the earth's surface is land, and how much is water?

About 30% of the earth's surface is land, and about 70% is water.

What is the highest point on earth?

The highest point is the top of Mount Everest in Asia: 29,028 feet (8848 meters) above sea level.

What is the lowest point?

The lowest point on the land is on the shore of the Dead Sea in Asia, 1299 feet (396 meters) below sea level.

Are the ocean floors much lower than that?

Yes, quite a bit. The average depth of the oceans is about 12,450 feet (3795 meters).

What is the deepest part of any ocean?

The deepest part is a valley called the Challenger Deep. It lies in the Mariana Trench, 36,198 feet (11,033 meters)—or nearly 7 miles (11.2 kilometers)—below the surface of the Pacific Ocean near Guam.

What is the inside of the earth like?

If we could see a cross section of the earth, we would see that the continents and ocean floors form a rocky, skinlike crust around the earth. Beneath this crust, the earth is a hot, lifeless ball of rock and metal.

What is the crust made of?

The crust is made of rocks that consist of oxygen, silicon, and various other chemicals.

But all the rocks aren't the same, are they?

No. They vary in chemical makeup, and they're grouped into categories according to how they were formed. *Igneous rocks* formed when melted rock cooled and hardened. *Sedimentary rocks* formed when bits of material settled in layers and hardened. *Metamorphic rocks* are the result of heat and pressure changing the form of igneous and sedimentary rocks.

What are the inner parts of the earth made of?

Scientists believe the very center, the *inner core*, is a ball-shaped mass of solid iron and nickel. Surrounding it is an *outer core*, probably of melted iron and nickel. The earth's *mantle* is a thick layer of solid rock that surrounds the outer core and lies just beneath the earth's crust.

How hot is the inside of the earth?

Scientists believe the average temperature of the upper part of the mantle ranges from about 1600° F (870° C) deep in the crust, to about 9000° F (5000° C) in the inner core.

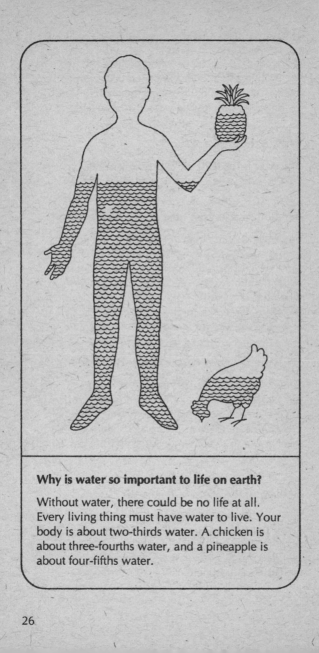

Why is water so important to life on earth?

Without water, there could be no life at all.
Every living thing must have water to live. Your
body is about two-thirds water. A chicken is
about three-fourths water, and a pineapple is
about four-fifths water.

How does that compare with the temperature on the earth's surface?

The average surface temperature is 57° F (14° C).

That temperature seems mild. What are the hottest and coldest temperatures ever recorded on the earth's surface?

The surface temperatures have ranged from a high of 136° F (58° C) at Àl Azīzīyah, Libya, to a low of −126.9° F (−88.3° C) at Vostok, in Antarctica.

Do the other planets have similar surface temperatures?

Not really. Mars is the closest, with an average temperature of −80° F (−62° C). Mercury and Venus are much hotter than earth, and all the remaining planets are colder.

Why is there such a difference in the surface temperatures of the planets?

The surface temperatures are related to the planets' distance from the sun. Mercury and Venus are closer to the sun than the earth is. All the other planets are farther from the sun.

How far is the sun from the earth?

The sun is about 93 million miles (150 million kilometers) away.

Is the air around the earth all oxygen?

Oh, no. In fact, oxygen makes up only about 21% of the earth's atmosphere.

Then what else is in the atmosphere?

Nitrogen makes up about 78% of the earth's atmosphere. The remaining 1% is mainly argon.

How far up does the earth's atmosphere go?

About 99% of the atmosphere lies within 100 miles (160 kilometers) of the earth. But bits of atmosphere exist up to 1000 miles (1600 kilometers) above it.

Is the temperature the same in all parts of the earth's atmosphere?

No. It varies at different altitudes. It drops to a low of about −135° F (−93° C) at 50 miles (80 kilometers) from earth. Beyond this point, the sun's radiation causes rapid increases in the temperature.

How hot is the hottest part of the atmosphere?

Scientists have recorded temperatures of over 2700° F (1480° C) in the layer of atmosphere that lies from 100 to 300 miles (160 to 480 kilometers) above the earth.

Why is it hot in the summer and cold in the winter in many places on earth?

The seasonal temperature changes on the earth's surface are caused by the earth's orbit around the sun and by the tilt of the earth's axis.

What is the *axis*?

The axis is an imaginary line that links the North and South poles. It tilts at an angle of about 23.5° from an upright position.

But how does that affect the temperature?

The tilt causes the sun's rays to hit the earth at different angles. For example, summer in the United States occurs when the northern half of the earth is tilted toward the sun. During winter, the northern half is tilted away from the sun.

What happens in the southern half of the earth during our summer?

During our summer, it is winter in the southern half of the earth. That's because when the northern half of the earth is tilted toward the sun, the southern half is tilted away from the sun. As the earth moves around the sun in its orbit, the seasons gradually change in both hemispheres.

The earth doesn't feel like it's moving at all. Is it going very fast as it travels around the sun?

Yes! It orbits at an average speed of 66,600 miles (107,200 kilometers) an hour.

What is the distance covered in one orbit?

One orbit of the earth consists of 595 million miles (958 million kilometers).

How long does it take the earth to return to the same place in its orbit?

One trip around the sun takes 365 days, 6 hours, 9 minutes, and 9.54 seconds. This is called one *sidereal* year, used in the calculations of astronomers.

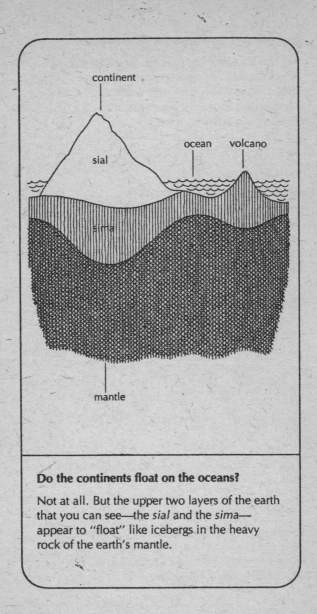

Do the continents float on the oceans?

Not at all. But the upper two layers of the earth that you can see—the *sial* and the *sima*— appear to "float" like icebergs in the heavy rock of the earth's mantle.

Is that how everyone measures a year?

No. The common year is the solar year, used for all practical purposes. The solar year is 365 days, 5 hours, 48 minutes, and 46 seconds. It is the time between two passages of the sun through the vernal equinox. The vernal equinox is the point at which the center of the sun moves across the celestial equator from north to south. It marks the beginning of spring in the Northern Hemisphere.

What causes night and day?

The spinning of the earth on its axis causes night and day. As the earth spins, one side is moving into the light of the sun—into daylight—and the other side is moving away from the sun's light—into darkness.

How many different ways does the earth move?

Three ways. It spins on its axis, it orbits around the sun, and it circles the Milky Way. There is, by the way, a possible fourth motion. This is the expanding universe theory, which says that each part of the universe is moving away from the other.

Does the moon move the same way the earth does?

The moon spins on its own axis and orbits around the earth. The moon and earth travel together around the sun and around the center of the Milky Way.

How far is the moon from the earth?

The distance varies because the moon's orbit is an oval shape. But the average distance between the center of the earth and the center of the moon is 238,857 miles (384,403 kilometers).

31

Compared to the earth, how big is the moon?

It's about a fourth as large in diameter as the earth.

That makes the moon much smaller than the sun, doesn't it?

Yes. The moon is about 400 times smaller in diameter than the sun. They appear to be similar in size because the moon is so much closer to the earth.

Is the moon made out of the same things as earth?

Scientists who have studied moon rocks and soil have found that many of the same minerals and gases that occur on earth are present on the moon. Moon samples have also helped scientists determine that the moon is about 4.6 billion years old.

How old is the earth?

It seems the earth is at least 4.5 billion years old. Many scientists think the earth and the moon were formed at the same time.

How do scientists think the earth and moon formed?

Most scientists believe the earth—and the rest of our solar system—developed from a huge cloud of gas and dust.

But the earth isn't just gas and dust now. What happened in between?

Well, again, there are several theories. Most of them assume that the earth began as a swirling body of gas, then changed into a ball of liquid, and finally cooled to form a solid crust.

After the earth cooled, did it look as it does today?

No. It was probably just a ball of rock surrounded by gases, with no oceans or other bodies of water.

How did the land areas and oceans develop?

Over the course of millions of years, heat—caused by radioactivity—and pressure made some elements sink toward the center of the earth and others to rise to the surface. The surface materials eventually became the ocean floors and land areas. Some of the chemicals in the earth combined to form water. The water collected in the low places on the earth and formed the oceans.

Were the oceans and continents always shaped as they are today?

No. In fact, many scientists who study the development of the earth believe that the continents were once a single land mass, surrounded by a single ocean.

Then how were the various continents formed?

According to a theory known as *continental drift*, the huge land mass began to split into two parts about 200 million years ago. One part then broke up into the continents of Africa, Antarctica, Australia, South America, and the Indian subcontinent. The other part broke up to form Eurasia and North America.

How long did it take for the continents to form?

It took millions of years for the land masses to form their present shapes and to drift into their present positions.

When did the continents stop drifting?

They haven't. According to another theory, the earth's outer surface is divided into rigid plates that are moving very slowly and carrying the continents and ocean floors with them.

What makes the plates move?

Scientists aren't sure. But one explanation is that currents of partially melted rock beneath the earth's crust cause the plates to move.

Do the plates all move in the same direction?

No. At certain places, the plates slide up against one another or collide.

What happens then?

Strains built up when two plates come together can cause an earthquake. Or one plate may pile up on top of another, forming mountains. The Himalayas in Asia, for example, were probably formed when the plate carrying India collided with the plate carrying Eurasia.

Were all the earth's mountains created by these collisions?

No. Other mountains, like the Rocky Mountains in the United States, formed when the earth's crust broke into huge blocks that then lifted or tilted. The Appalachian Mountains are an example of mountains created in places where the earth's surface wrinkled into wavelike folds.

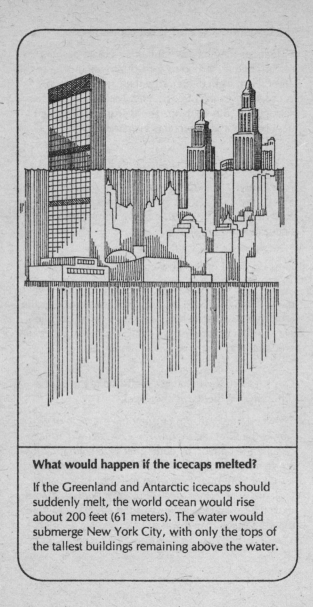

What would happen if the icecaps melted?

If the Greenland and Antarctic icecaps should suddenly melt, the world ocean would rise about 200 feet (61 meters). The water would submerge New York City, with only the tops of the tallest buildings remaining above the water.

What about volcanoes? What causes them?

Volcanoes may be the result of one plate pushing under another and being forced into the mantle of the earth. Heat from deep inside the earth may then cause some of the plate to melt. Molten lava and ash shoot out of the volcano. These eruptions produce new islands and mountains even today.

So the earth is still changing, isn't it?

Absolutely! The earth is in a constant state of change. Not all the changes are as sudden and dramatic as an earthquake or a volcano, though. Some changes occur much more slowly.

How do some of the slow changes occur?

Well, take the weathering of rocks. This occurs when things like water, ice, or growing plants break up the rocks into smaller particles. Erosion may then take place when water, wind, or glaciers move the weathered material from one place to another.

Can these gradual changes really make much of a difference in the earth's surface?

They certainly can. An outstanding example of erosion is the Grand Canyon. The Colorado River has created the canyon by cutting through solid rock to erode a path more than 1 mile (1.6 kilometers) deep. It's taken millions of years for the Grand Canyon to look the way it does today. But, nevertheless, things like erosion have helped make the earth a very different place than it was at first.

Fascinating animals

Does anyone know how many kinds of animals there are in the world?

Scientists have identified nearly a million different kinds of animals so far, and they discover new kinds all the time. The animal world includes a tremendous variety of insects, fishes, birds, mammals, reptiles, and other creatures.

Is there one animal group that is much bigger than all the others?

Yes. There are at least 800,000 different kinds of insects alone. That compares with about 21,000 kinds of fish, more than 9,000 kinds of birds, and about 4,000 kinds of mammals.

What is the total insect population?

It's impossible to know exactly. But the estimated number of individual insects in the world is staggering. There are at least four times as many insects in the world as there are all other animals combined. Scientists estimate that in every square mile (2.6 square kilometers) of land, there are as many insects as there are people in the entire world.

Are insects the smallest animals?

They are among the smallest. Most of them are less than .25 inch (6.4 millimeters) long. But the smallest animals are protozoans, which consist of just one cell. Most can be seen only with a microscope.

Animals vary in so many ways. Are there certain things that all animals have in common?

Yes. All animals eat plants or other animals for food. And nearly all of them move about through their own power. These two characteristics are what make animals different from plants.

Do most animals have legs to move themselves about?

Yes. Many of the most familiar animals—dogs, cats, horses, and many others—have four legs. Birds have two legs, insects have six, and spiders have eight. Some animals have many more. A centipede, for example, may have more than 300 legs. Of course, there are other animals—such as fish—that have no legs at all.

Why do animals' legs come in so many different shapes and sizes?

An animal's legs—and many of its other body parts—fit the animal's particular environmental needs.

What does *environment* mean?

Environment is an animal's or plant's surroundings. A frog, for example, lives both on land and in water. So its muscular hind legs enable it both to leap about on land and to swim expertly in the water. Some insects have sticky pads on the ends of their legs that allow them to walk on walls and ceilings. Many land animals have long legs for running.

What animal is the fastest runner?

The cheetah is the fastest runner. It can run more than 70 miles per hour (110 kilometers per hour).

Does that make it the fastest of all animals?

No. Certain kinds of birds are much faster. Diving, the duck hawk and the golden eagle can speed along at 180 miles per hour (290 kilometers per hour), a rate that makes them the fastest animals in the world.

How does that compare with water animals?

As a group, water animals are slower than birds and land animals. But the barracuda and sailfish can swim as fast as 30 miles per hour (48 kilometers per hour).

Are there any insects that can fly as fast as birds?

Some insects actually can fly faster than some birds.

I've heard that people can wrestle alligators. How is that possible?

It is possible to control alligators in a simple way. They have powerful jaws that are strong enough to crush cattle bones. But, once the jaws are shut, they can be held closed by a person's hands.

What is the fastest insect?

Probably the fastest insect is the dragonfly, which can reach an estimated speed of 60 miles per hour (97 kilometers per hour). There are other insects that don't fly as fast but can go a long distance without stopping. Butterflies, for example, have enough energy stored in their bodies to fly more than 100 miles (160 kilometers).

Are there any birds that can't fly?

Yes, several kinds, including ostriches and penguins.

Then how do they move around in their environment?

Ostriches use their long legs to walk—or to run—from place to place. Ostriches can run at about 40 miles per hour (64 kilometers per hour). Penguins waddle clumsily on land and use their wings to swim underwater. There are other kinds of birds that can swim underwater faster than some fish.

What's a fast swimming bird?

The loon is a champion underwater swimmer. It can dive deep into the water and catch fish that aren't fast enough to escape.

If there are birds that swim, are there also some kinds of fish that fly?

Yes. One of them, the flying hatchet fish, uses its side fins to take off from the surface of the water and fly. But it can go only about 10 feet (3 meters). There are other fish that can "walk" considerable distances.

A walking fish? That's hard to believe. What kind is it?

The walking catfish can swim out of a lake and use its tail and fins to crawl to another nearby lake if it wants to. It can live for days out of water.

Are there other animals that travel in unusual ways?

Yes. One of the most unusual is a lizard that lives in Asia and the East Indies. It's called the flying dragon. This reptile has folds of skin that it spreads out like wings to glide from tree to tree.

Are some animals known for traveling great distances?

Certain kinds of animals make regular trips, or *migrate*, to find food, avoid cold weather, or bear their young. These migrations may cover hundreds, or even thousands, of miles.

What are some examples of animals that migrate?

Certain kinds of deer and butterflies migrate. And there are eels that live in European rivers and swim thousands of miles to the western Atlantic Ocean to lay their eggs.

What animal makes the longest migration?

A bird called the arctic tern migrates the farthest. Every August, terns fly from the northern islands of the Arctic Ocean to Antarctica. The following June, they fly back home to the Arctic, completing a round trip of about 22,000 miles (35,400 kilometers).

What about animals that don't migrate? Do they tend to stay in one area most of their lives?

Yes. A few kinds of animals—sea fans, for example—stay fixed in one place most of their lives. But the majority of animals move about within a home "territory."

Does the territory have definite boundaries?

In many cases, yes, though people may not be able to see the boundaries. A snowshoe rabbit, for example, may never venture more than about .25 mile (.4 kilometer) from its birthplace. Even if chased by another animal, it will run to its boundary, then turn and run in another direction, never going beyond its limits.

Do most animals build some sort of home?

Many do, but there are others that never build homes. Some animals—many of them birds—may build homes only to raise their young.

Do all birds build the same kind of nest?

No. And not all birds build the sorts of nests that are familiar to many of us. The flamingo, for example, forms piles of mud into a sort of cone-shaped structure. The tailorbird of India and Africa uses its bill as a needle and sews leaves together with long strips of grass or fibers. Certain kinds of swifts in Malaya build nests almost entirely out of their saliva, which hardens to form a crust.

What do the homes of some other animals look like?

Animal homes vary greatly in their form and complexity. A bear may simply take over a cave for its home and never actually "build" anything. A beaver, on the other hand, carefully constructs a home of sticks and mud with an underwater entrance that keeps away its enemies. Clams, oysters, and some other water animals carry their shell homes around with them. Some of the more interesting homes are the nests built by ants.

What do ants' nests look like?

The more elaborate ones consist of several underground rooms connected by passageways that spread out over an area as large as 1 acre (.4 hectare). Some of the rooms are "nurseries" where eggs are laid or hatched, or young ants are tended. The ants use other rooms to store grain or to hold trash.

How do ants manage to build such complicated homes?

They dig into the soil and carry out the dirt, bit by bit. One reason ants are such successful builders is that they have amazing strength.

How strong is an ant?

An ant can lift 50 times its own weight. To be as strong as an ant, a 175-pound (79-kilogram) man would have to be able to lift more than 4 short tons (3.6 metric tons)—with his teeth.

Does an ant have muscles?

Yes. All insects have at least several hundred muscles. In fact, caterpillars have from 2,000 to 4,000 muscles. Humans, by comparison, have fewer than 700.

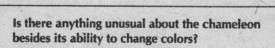

Is there anything unusual about the chameleon besides its ability to change colors?

Yes. In fact, its ability to change colors is not unique. Many other lizards can do that. But chameleons are able to do many unusual things. They have bulging eyes that can look right and left at the same time. Their feet grasp like fingers, not like claws, and their tails curl up. Perhaps most interesting, their sticky tongues are about as long as their bodies and swiftly shoot out to catch food.

Could you say ants do many of the same things that people do?

Yes. In fact, we call ants "social insects" because they live together in groups and behave in some ways that are remarkably similar to human behavior.

Are there other kinds of social insects?

Yes. Other kinds include termites, many kinds of bees, and some wasps.

Do other kinds of animals besides social insects live in groups?

Of course. Birds may travel together in flocks, and fish swim in groups called *schools*. Some mammals live together in herds. And many animals take part in a kind of social life that involves finding a mate and raising a family.

How do some animals go about finding a mate?

Animals have many interesting ways of finding a mate. Fireflies flash special signals. Some male birds and fish do elaborate courtship dances to impress females. Birds may also use special courtship songs, and frogs and grasshoppers make distinctive sounds to call a mate. A female gypsy moth that wants to mate releases a scent into the air that can be detected by a male moth up to 1 mile (1.6 kilometers) away.

Are some animals better than others at raising families?

Definitely. Some animals, including most insects and fish, ignore their young completely. On the other hand, monkeys are quite affectionate toward their offspring and carefully teach them how to get along in the world. And some animals have special ways to make sure their young survive under harsh conditions.

What kinds of harsh conditions?

Well, emperor penguins are a good example. They live in the severe cold of Antarctica. They lay their eggs on their toes, then tuck their toes and eggs underneath themselves. The eggs hatch among the warm feathers of the penguin's underside. The young penguins remain there, snug and warm, until they are large enough to survive in the cold.

How do other kinds of animals survive extreme cold?

Animals have various ways to deal with the cold. Polar bears and some other arctic animals have thick, furry coats to keep warm. The feet of an arctic bird called the ptarmigan stay warm because they're covered with feathers, unlike the feet of most other birds. Some animals simply avoid the cold by hibernating.

What does *hibernating* mean?

Hibernating means greatly increased sleeping during the wintry season. Many hibernating animals find a cave or other warm place for their long rest. Some animals sleep straight through the cold weather; others take "naps" and remain in a lazy state. Bats, frogs, skunks, woodchucks, bees, and many other kinds of animals hibernate.

Don't they starve while they're asleep?

No. Many of them eat so much during the summer that they become quite fat. During hibernation, their body uses the stored fat as food.

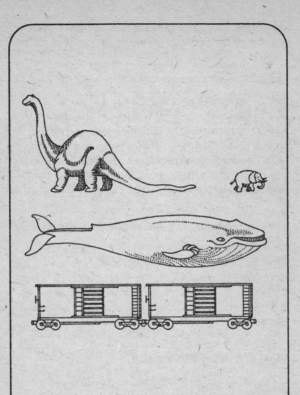

What is the biggest animal?

The biggest of all animals is the blue whale. It can grow up to 100 feet (30 meters) long, or longer than two railroad boxcars. It weighs up to 100 short tons (91 metric tons). It is larger than the hugest of all dinosaurs and much bigger than the elephant, which is the largest land animal.

Are there animals that hibernate during the summer?

No, none hibernate during the summer. Hibernation is a term used only for winter sleeping. But in the summer, many animals *estivate,* the correct word for summer sleeping. Certain snails, snakes, and lizards that live in hot places estivate in mud or other cool spots.

How do other animals adjust to a hot climate?

Like the animals that survive extreme cold, many animals that live in hot places have special features to cope with the climate. For example, desert foxes and mice have long ears and tails through which much of their body heat escapes. Other animals have special features to cope with environmental factors other than climate.

Which special features?

Well, many fish that live in the deep, dark parts of the ocean have large eyes and special light organs that flash on and off. There are other fish that live in mountain streams with currents so rough that few other creatures can live in them. These fish survive because they have suction organs that enable them to hold onto rocks in the stream.

What about defense? Do most animals fight to protect themselves?

No. Many simply try to escape. Some long-legged animals like giraffes and kangaroos can flee from their enemies at high speeds. Other animals are equipped with special kinds of "armor" or other coverings that provide safety. Two of the more interesting animal defenses are protective coloration and resemblance.

What is protective coloration?

Animals with protective coloration have body colors that make them seem to disappear against their background. Many kinds of birds, for example, have speckled feathers that make them hard to see. In much the same way, a tiger's striped coat blends in with the tall, shadowy grass it walks through.

Does protective resemblance work in a similar way?

Yes. But with protective resemblance, an animal has a body shape, as well as color, that looks like something in its environment. There are various insects, for example, that look like thorns, dead leaves, bird droppings, or twigs. There are some fish—stonefish—that look like rocks, and other fish look like water plants. Protective coloration and protective resemblance are excellent safeguards against *predators*, or animals that kill and eat other animals.

Are all animals predators?

No. All animals need food, but not all kill for it.

Can animals taste their food?

Many of them can. But not all of them have a tongue for tasting. A butterfly tastes with its feet. And some kinds of fish are believed to have taste buds all over their skin.

What about some of the other senses? Can animals hear, see, and smell like humans?

Some animals don't have all the human senses, or the animals' senses are poorly developed. But certain creatures have some much better developed senses than humans. Certain kinds of dogs, for example, have a sense of smell so keen they can detect the scent of a person buried under 20 feet (6 meters) of snow. And a dragonfly can see a gnat flying 18 feet (5.5 meters) away.

What are some of the smarter animals?

The smarter animals are the flesh-eating mammals like cats and dogs; the ocean mammals, including dolphins and whales; and apes and monkeys. All these can learn to solve problems and do other things that show much intelligence. But none is more intelligent than the most complex animals of all—humans.

The human side of life

The human body is a very complicated thing. How does the body work to maintain life?

The human body is made up of many different but related systems. Each system is responsible for a particular bodily function. Together, these systems work to maintain life.

How do these systems work to maintain life?

Every system in the human body is involved in one or more of three tasks:

1. getting energy from food
2. using that energy for all respiration, nerve impulse energy, or muscle contraction energy
3. generating offspring.

The successful completion of these three tasks enables the human body to use the fuel it needs to reproduce itself and to carry on the other activities we normally associate with the word *life*.

What are the main systems in the human body?

The skeletal system supports the body, and the muscular system enables the body to move. The respiratory system helps the body obtain necessary oxygen and dispose of harmful carbon dioxide. The digestive system breaks food down into chemical parts that the body can then use as fuel. The circulatory system carries these chemicals to all body cells. The endocrine system uses hormones as chemical messengers to start and stop many bodily activities at the correct time. The urinary system helps the body to dispose of poisonous wastes. The reproductive system enables the body to produce offspring. And all of these systems are under the control of the nervous system and its controlling organ, the brain.

How many bones are there in the skeletal system?

There are 206 bones in the human skeletal system. They are composed primarily of calcium. Tough cords called ligaments connect the bones.

Are all the bones alike?

No. The bony human framework is divided into two components. The first, called the axial skeleton, is made up of the skull, ribcage, and vertebral column. The second, called the appendicular skeleton, is made up of the body's limbs.

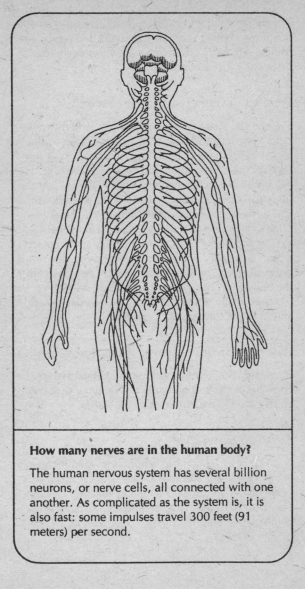

How many nerves are in the human body?

The human nervous system has several billion neurons, or nerve cells, all connected with one another. As complicated as the system is, it is also fast: some impulses travel 300 feet (91 meters) per second.

Is the skull made up of one large bone?

No. The skull is made up of a number of tightly fitting bones, organized into two main parts.

What are these parts, and how many bones does each have?

The two parts of the skull are called the cranium and the face. The cranium is made up of 8 bones—1 frontal, 2 temporals, 2 parietals, 1 occipital, 1 sphenoid, and 1 ethmoid. The face contains 14 bones, including 2 maxillae (upper jaw) and the hinged mandible (lower jaw). Other facial bones are the palatine (back of the mouth), the nasal (nose), and the zygomatics (cheekbones).

Are the bones of the skull the most complicated part of the skeletal system?

While the skull is a highly complex system of bones, the most complicated part of the skeletal system is the vertebral column.

How many bones make up the vertebral column?

Twenty-six bones make up the vertebral column.

What do these bones do?

Seven cervical vertebrae form the neck. There are 12 thoracic vertebrae that have ribs attached to them. Five lumbar vertebrae connect the upper body with the lower body. In adults, a single bone called the sacrum connects the two bony portions of the hips. Finally, the coccyx (tailbone) is a structure made up of 4 fused bones.

All of the bones described to this point are part of the axial skeleton. What are some of the bones that are part of the appendicular skeleton?

The upper appendicular skeleton is made up of the pectoral girdle (shoulder) and, suspended from it, the arm and hand bones. The lower appendicular skeleton is made up of the pelvic girdle and, attached to it, the lower limbs.

What enables the body to move portions of the skeletal system?

The muscular system enables the body to move portions of the skeletal system.

How many muscles are there in the human body?

The human body contains more than 500 muscles.

What are muscles made of?

Each muscle is made of long cells called muscle fibers. Each muscle fiber is made of many thin fibers that slide on one another.

How do muscles work?

When the nerves attached to muscles trigger muscle contraction, the muscle fibers shorten to about half their normal length. When a muscle is not in the state of contraction, it relaxes.

Are all of the muscles in the human body alike?

No. There are three separate kinds of muscles in the human body: voluntary, involuntary, and cardiac.

What do the three kinds of muscles do?

Voluntary muscles are responsible for bodily movements and posture. They are called "voluntary" because we consciously control their contractions.

Involuntary muscles are part of the digestive and endocrine organs. Their contractions are controlled by parts of the brain that operate at below-conscious levels; that is, we are not aware of these contractions.

Cardiac muscle fibers control the heartbeat. These fibers are interconnected so as to allow a uniform spread of the electrical signals that stimulate the heartbeat.

What is the job performed by the heart?

The heart is a fist-sized muscular pump. Its job is to maintain a steady circulation of blood through the body.

How does the heart do its job?

Electrical impulses from the portion of the heart called the pacemaker cause the heart muscle to contract (systolic stage) and relax (diastolic stage) at a rate of about 70 beats per minute.

How much blood does the average human body contain, and how fast does it circulate?

The average adult human body contains about 5 quarts (4.75 liters) of blood. The body's entire supply of blood circulates approximately once per minute.

What part does blood play in the functioning of the human body?

Blood transports food and oxygen to all cells. It also

removes the waste products created by the continuous process of cell metabolism. Blood is an important part of the body's fight against disease, since certain blood cells are able to destroy harmful bacteria and viruses.

What is blood made of?

Blood is made of a solid part and a liquid part. The liquid part, a watery solution called plasma, consists of carbohydrates, fats, and proteins.

But what about the solid part?

The solid part of blood is made up primarily of three kinds of cells—white blood cells (leukocytes), platelets (thrombocytes), and red blood cells (erythrocytes).

What does each of these three kinds of cells do?

White blood cells attack bacteria, viruses, and other infections that invade the body. Platelets work in combination with fibery proteins in plasma to form the blood clots that seal injuries. Red blood cells carry oxygen to other cells throughout the body.

How do red blood cells carry oxygen to other cells?

Red blood cells contain a red protein called hemoglobin. Oxygen combines with hemoglobin. This is a vital function, since every minute the human body needs about 250 cubic centimeters of oxygen in order to survive.

From where does the oxygen the body needs come?

Oxygen comes into the body via respiration.

How does the respiratory system work?

The basic activity of the respiratory system is breathing. Breathing is a rhythmic activity that draws oxygen-rich air into the lungs and expels air loaded with carbon dioxide from them.

What regulates breathing?

A large, dome-shaped muscle called the diaphragm plays a key role in regulating breathing. This muscle separates the chest cavity from the abdominal cavity. As the diaphragm contracts, the chest cavity expands, sucking air into the lungs. When the diaphragm relaxes, the chest cavity contracts. Pressure builds in the chest cavity, and this pressure deflates the lungs.

How does the body use the oxygen in air?

At the end of long air passages in the lungs there are spongy sacs called alveoli. The alveoli are surrounded by many capillaries, the smallest blood vessels in the body. The capillaries are connected to veins. The walls of capillaries are so thin that molecules of oxygen and carbon dioxide can pass in and out.

Air breathed into the lungs collects in the alveoli. Blood flowing through the capillaries absorbs life-giving oxygen from the air in the alveoli and carries the oxygen throughout the body. At the same time, the blood deposits in the alveoli the carbon dioxide that is the waste product of the body's use of oxygen. This carbon dioxide is removed from the body in the air that is exhaled from the lungs.

Is breathing important for any reason other than the exchange of oxygen and carbon dioxide within the body?

Absolutely. We could not speak without breathing. At the top of the trachea, the tube that connects the mouth and nasal cavity with the lungs, there is an organ called the larynx, commonly known as the voice box. It contains a set of muscles called the vocal cords. Sounds are vibrations produced by the passage of air over the vocal cords.

So, the respiratory system provides the fuel that keeps the body alive?

Well, the respiratory system provides *some* of the necessary fuel. The rest comes from the food we eat.

That's right, food is important. How does the body use food?

The body uses food through the functioning of the digestive system.

How does the digestive system work?

Digestion begins the moment we put food into the mouth. As we chew, salivary glands there release enzymes that begin the chemical process of reducing starch into sugars. The tongue continues the process by helping us to swallow chewed food, which travels down the 10-inch-long (250-millimeter) esophagus into the stomach. Enzymes and acids in the stomach continue to break the food down into the various chemicals the body needs.

But how does the food and its chemicals get from the stomach to the other parts of the body?

The stomach churns and stores the digested food, or chyme. Periodically, the stomach releases small amounts of chyme into the 10-inch-long (250-

millimeter) duodenum. The duodenum is the first part of the small intestine.

What happens when chyme enters the intestine?

The walls of the 22-foot-long (660-centimeter) small intestine are covered by small, fingerlike projections containing blood vessels. As the chyme moves through the small intestine, the blood vessels absorb necessary nutrients for distribution through the body.

How is chyme "moved" through the small intestine?

The small intestine is a muscular organ. Muscles in the wall of the small intestine contract in a wavelike motion called peristalsis. This motion moves the chyme to the ileum of the small intestine and on into the cecum. The cecum is the beginning of the large intestine.

What does the large intestine do?

By the time chyme gets to the 5-foot-long (150-centimeter) large intestine, the bloodstream has absorbed most of the nutrients. The main function of the large intestine is to remove water from the remains of the chyme. The final product of this process is the feces, which are then eliminated from the body.

Are other body organs part of the digestive system?

Yes. The liver stores nutrients and releases them as the body needs them. The liver also removes poisons from the blood and turns them into a liquid called bile. The gall bladder stores bile and releases it into the digestive tract for elimination from the body. And the pancreas produces the digestive enzymes that break food down into nutrients.

Why is it difficult to taste food when the nose is stopped up?

The sense of taste is partially in the taste buds, but it is also closely related to the sense of smell—in the nose. In fact, some experts believe that taste sensations are really sensations of odor associated with certain tastes. Supposing you had a stuffy nose. If you closed your eyes and bit an apple and a raw potato, you would have trouble telling them apart by taste.

What about the other important systems in the human body?

The endocrine system is a complex arrangement of glands that produce, store, and release, when needed, a variety of chemicals called hormones. These hormones act as chemical messengers that start and stop the operation of many of the body's organs.

Closely related to the endocrine system is the reproductive system. It enables the human species to perpetuate itself through the generation of offspring.

Finally, the urinary system works to eliminate various harmful wastes from the body. The key organs of the urinary system are the two kidneys, which serve as filters for the blood as it travels through the circulatory system.

So all of this is going on inside of me. Is the body doing anything else?

It sure is. Your eyes are seeing light and objects. Your ears are hearing sounds. Your nose is sensing smells. And you are tasting and touching things. While other systems within the body keep it operating, the sensory system works to help you interpret the world outside.

The jobs done by the organs of the sensory system seem complex. How do these organs work?

Each of the organs that is part of the sensory system has specialized parts that help it to do its specific job. The eye, for example, is made up of a clear cornea, a pupil, and a lens. These three organs permit light rays to enter and also focus them for optic nerve reception.

Through a complex system, the ear registers the vibrations that make up sound waves. The system includes the eardrum, three delicate bones in the middle ear (the malleus, the incus, and the stapes), an opening called the oval window, and a fluid-filled organ called the cochlea. The ear also serves as the body's organ of balance through the movement of fluid and minute particles in a part of the ear called the semicircular canals. The cochlear nerve receives the vibrations for both sound and for information about balance.

What about the senses of smell, taste, and touch?

All three of these sensory activities depend in one way or another on contact between various nerve endings and "sensations" from outside the body. Olfactory nerves located at the top of the nasal cavity permit you to distinguish smells. Taste buds located on the tongue are connected to sensory nerves that distinguish tastes. Nerve endings close to the surface of the skin act as sensation receptors that activate the sense of touch.

This all seems complicated. How does the body make these many systems work together?

The nervous system controls all the other systems of the body. And the brain directs the nervous system.

How complex is the nervous system?

Very complex. Actually, the nervous system is made up of three subsystems: the central nervous system, the peripheral nervous system, and the autonomic nervous system. Each of these subsystems is responsible for a particular set of bodily activities.

What does each subsystem do?

The central nervous system, which consists of the brain and the spinal cord, is the main controlling unit of the nervous system. The peripheral nervous system consists of the cranial and spinal nerves and controls the body's motor (movement) activities and sensory activities (sight, hearing, smell, taste, and touch). The autonomic nervous system controls the activities of the stomach, intestines, and other abdominal organs. The brain directs the autonomic nervous system at below-conscious levels.

How does the nervous system work?

Nerve information is made up largely of a series of minute electrical impulses sent to the brain for interpretation and then to the muscles for action. Incidentally, nerve impulses can travel in one direction only. Impulses directed toward the brain travel along sensory nerves. Impulses from the brain travel along motor nerves.

How does the brain control the body's activities?

The brain is divided into several different parts, each responsible for control of a different set of bodily functions. The cerebrum controls the so-called "higher" mental activities. These consist of memory, motivation, and awareness. The so-called "lower" mental activities such as balance and breathing are controlled by the pons, cerebellum, and medulla.

So, all in all, the human body is a marvelous structure, isn't it?

Absolutely. It is an incredibly well-organized and beautifully managed system. We are still not sure, however, how the human body begins to live; nor do we know how and why it grows and dies. Even with today's scientific advances, the reason the human body works remains a mystery.

Everywhere — plants!

How many different kinds of plants are there?

There are probably more than 350,000 different kinds of plants. More than half are what we call *flowering plants*—plants that produce flowers, fruits, and seeds. But the plant kingdom also includes simple plants like algae and molds, as well as mosses, ferns, and other nonflowering varieties.

What is an example of a tiny plant?

A one-celled plant called a *diatom* is among the smallest.

How small is a diatom?

A diatom is so small, it can't be seen without a

microscope. A single drop of water may contain as many as 500 of these tiny plants.

What is the biggest plant?

The biggest plant is the giant sequoia tree, found only in California. In fact, the sequoias are the largest living things in the world.

How big are the bigger sequoias?

Some sequoias measure more than 30 feet (9 meters) wide and more than 290 feet (88 meters) tall. That's about as tall as a 30-story building.

The sequoias must be very old to have grown so huge. How old are they?

Many of the sequoias date from 1500 BC. But the sequoias aren't the oldest of all plants.

They aren't? Then what are the oldest plants?

Bristlecone pine trees are the oldest of all plants. There's a bristlecone pine in California that began growing 4,000 to 5,000 years ago. That tree is the oldest living thing on earth.

When did plants first grow on earth?

No one knows exactly when the first plants appeared on earth. But scientists have found fossils of plants that lived more than 3 billion years ago. It's possible that plants similar to algae lived in the ocean as long ago as 4 billion years.

When did plants first start growing on land?

The first land plants existed about 435 million years ago.

What did they look like?

The earliest land plants had a simple structure of horizontal stems with upright branches.

What were some of the other early plants?

Club mosses, horsetails, and seed ferns, the ancestors of modern ferns, began to grow in many parts of the world about 400 million years ago.

When did the kinds of trees and other plants common today start developing?

Familiar trees like oaks and maples came into existence about 130 million years ago, and cone-bearing trees had existed long before that. But it wasn't until about 26 million years ago that most of the earth's trees and other plants resembled their present-day descendants.

It's hard to imagine what the world was like 26 million years ago. Were there animals then?

There were many kinds of animals at that time. But don't forget the plants. They were there, too. Without the earth's plant life, animals wouldn't exist today.

Animals—that includes people—depend on plants for food. Almost everything we eat is either a plant or the product of an animal that ate plants. In most cases, we don't eat an entire plant, but rather a specific part of it.

Like the fruit of an apple tree?

Right. We eat many kinds of fruits. And when we eat spinach or lettuce, we're eating plant leaves. A stalk of celery or a spear of asparagus is a plant stem. Carrots and beets are roots. We even eat flowers. Heads of broccoli and cauliflower are actually clusters of flower buds. But the most important plant foods are seeds.

What kinds of seeds?

Corn, rice, and wheat are three of the most important seed foods.

Why are they so important?

Because these grains provide the chief source of food for most of the people in the world. In fact, rice alone is the chief food for about half the world's people. Sometimes, seeds are eaten indirectly, as when wheat and other grains are milled to make flour for bread and other foods. And meat and dairy products come from animals that eat grain.

What else do plants provide us with besides food?

Plants provide us with a great variety of raw materials, and many important medicines—penicillin, for one—are made from plants.

What kinds of raw materials do plants provide?

Lumber, paper, cork, and turpentine are among the many products that come from trees. Cotton and other plants provide fibers that are woven into cloth and made into string and rope. Plants are also the source of many fuels.

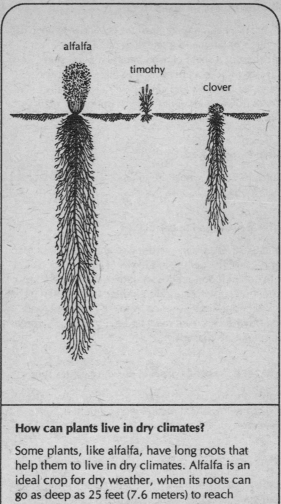

How can plants live in dry climates?

Some plants, like alfalfa, have long roots that help them to live in dry climates. Alfalfa is an ideal crop for dry weather, when its roots can go as deep as 25 feet (7.6 meters) to reach water. The roots of other common forage crops extend a much shorter distance.

Like wood?

Yes. Many people burn wood as fuel. But those who use coal, natural gas, and oil are also using plant products. These three fuels were formed millions of years ago by the action of pressure on layers of decayed plants.

Is there anything else that plants give us that we couldn't do without?

Yes, indeed. In addition to all these other things, plants give us the oxygen we breathe.

How do they do that?

The oxygen-giving function of plants is part of something called the *cycle of nature*, which links plants and animals. Plants make their own food, and, in the process, they give off oxygen as a by-product. Animals breathe in the oxygen and exhale carbon dioxide. The plants, in turn, need the carbon dioxide to make more food, and the cycle continues.

So, in a way, plants are just as dependent on animals as animals are dependent on plants, right?

Right.

How, specifically, does a plant make its own food?

The food-making process, which is called *photosynthesis*, takes place in the leaves of most plants. The leaves are like food "factories." Sunlight provides the energy needed for photosynthesis. The leaves absorb sunlight and use the energy to combine carbon dioxide from the air with water and minerals from the soil. This process produces food.

How does the plant use this food?

The plant uses the food to grow and to develop its various parts. An apple, for example, is produced by the food-making activity of about 50 leaves of an apple tree.

How does a plant like a cactus make food? It doesn't have leaves, does it?

It certainly does. The sharp, prickly spines of a cactus are actually leaves. But, in the case of a cactus, photosynthesis takes place in the fleshy green stem.

The spines of a cactus are really leaves?

Yes. Leaves come in many shapes and sizes. On some plants, they're broad and flat. On others—pine trees, for example—they're like needles. The biggest leaves, found on raffia palm trees, can grow to be 50 feet (15 meters) long and 8 feet (2.4 meters) wide.

Are there any plants that don't have leaves?

Yes. Many plants, including various kinds of fungi and molds, don't have leaves.

Then how do they make food?

That depends on the plant. Some of them get food by attaching themselves to other live vegetation. Others—including mushrooms—live off decaying plants and animals.

So even those leafless plants couldn't get along if it weren't for the leaves of other plants, could they?

That's right.

Why do the leaves of some trees change color and fall off in autumn?

Leaves contain various coloring substances. One example is chlorophyll, the pigment that makes leaves green. In late summer, a process begins that cuts off the supply of water to the leaves, and the chlorophyll in them breaks down. Then other colors—the reds, yellows, and browns hidden by the chlorophyll—show up. Eventually, the lack of water causes the leaf to die and fall off the tree.

Are leaves the most important part of most plants?

The leaves are obviously quite important. But they work with other plant parts in a complete system that provides for the plant's development.

What are the other main plant parts?

In flowering plants, which are the most common kinds, the main parts in addition to the leaves are the root, stem, and flower.

What do the roots do for the plant?

Roots hold the plant in the soil. They also absorb the water and dissolved soil minerals that the plant needs to make food.

Why are stems important?

In most plants, the stems support the leaves and flowers and hold them up to the sunlight. Stems carry water and minerals from the roots up to the leaves and also carry food from the leaves back to the rest of the plant.

Do all stems grow straight up?

No. Stems have various forms. They are the trunks, branches, and twigs of a tree. Some stems, like those of potatoes, grow partly underground. The fleshy part of a cactus is its stem. Some plants, like lettuce, have stems so short they're hard to see.

There are many kinds of flowers, too, aren't there?

There certainly are. Most of us think of flowers with colored petals and pleasant fragrances. But some flowers—the swamp marigold, for example—have no petals at all, and others give off a terrible odor. The flower of the western skunk cabbage smells like its namesake.

How do flowers range in size?

The smallest flower is the bloom of the duckweed plant, barely visible to the naked eye. The largest is the giant rafflesia, which grows in Indonesia and can measure as large as 3 feet (91 centimeters) across and can weigh as much as 15 pounds (7 kilograms).

Why do plants have flowers?

Flowers are important because they contain the plant's reproductive system. The reproductive system is what forms fruits and seeds. The seeds, in turn, produce new plants.

Do big seeds produce big plants and small seeds produce small plants?

That sounds logical, but there's no such rule. The size of the seed has nothing to do with the eventual size of the plant. Huge redwood trees, for example, grow from seeds that are only one-sixteenth of an inch (1.6 millimeters) long.

If a seed is planted upside down, will the roots grow up out of the soil and the stem down into the ground?

No. A plant's roots almost always grow downward—toward the source of gravity—and its stem almost always begins growing upward—away from the source of gravity. Those kinds of plant movements are called *tropisms*. Other tropisms may cause a plant to bend toward a light source or may cause a plant's roots to grow toward a source of water.

How are the seeds that grow all over the world planted?

People plant many seeds in gardens and on farms, but most plants grow from seeds that were never touched by people.

Never touched by people? Then how do the seeds get into the soil?

First, seeds are scattered by one of a variety of ways. Then, if they land in a place where there's enough moisture and the temperature is right, they may eventually sprout into new plants.

What are some of the ways seeds are scattered?

Some seeds have winglike parts that enable the wind to carry them. Others float on water. Some seeds stick to animals, or animals eat the seeds and then deposit them as part of body wastes. Some plants are constructed so that they discharge their seeds at the slightest touch.

So some seeds have features that almost guarantee they'll get from one place to another, don't they?

That's right. And these seed features are examples of how over thousands of years plants have adapted to guarantee their own survival.

Adapted? What does that mean?

Adapt means "change to fit a certain set of conditions." Over the course of thousands of years, plants have changed in many ways and have developed characteristics that allow them to survive under varying conditions. Some plants even have characteristics that protect them against plant-eating animals.

How can plants protect themselves against animals?

The thorns and spines that grow on certain plants are examples of the kinds of features plants have developed to protect themselves against animals. Some plants—poison ivy, for example—contain liquids that keep animals away.

So some plants are actually dangerous, aren't they?

Yes. Several are dangerous or harmful. Some plants cause diseases like hay fever and asthma. Weeds can crowd out other useful plants, and various fungi are the origin of destructive plant diseases. One group of unusual plants is particularly dangerous to insects.

Why are they dangerous to insects?

Because they're plants that *eat* insects.

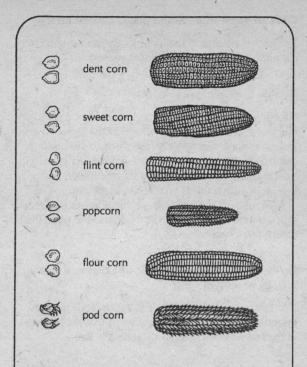

dent corn

sweet corn

flint corn

popcorn

flour corn

pod corn

What is popcorn?

Popcorn is just one of six kinds of corn: dent, sweet, flint, flour, pod, and popcorn. Each has its particular use, but popcorn is the only kind that will pop when heated. All the others will simply crack or dry up.

Popcorn is an American "fun food." Dent and flint corn are called "field corn" because we feed them to animals. Sweet corn is a food corn. Flour corn and pod corn are not grown commercially in North America.

What are some examples of plants that eat insects?

The pitcher plant and the Venus's-flytrap are two of the most interesting insect-eating plants.

How do these plants eat insects?

Pitcher plants have tube-shaped leaves that collect rain water. Sweet substances around the rims of the leaves attract insects. When the creature ventures down the tube, tiny, downward-pointing hairs keep it from escaping. Eventually, the insect drowns, and special digestive fluids enable the plant to digest it.

A Venus's-flytrap has hairy, hinged leaves that snap shut when an insect lands on the hairs. The plant then digests the insect.

Do these plants eat insects because they can't make food by photosynthesis?

No. They use photosynthesis to make food, but the insects provide certain vital minerals that are lacking in the soil where these plants generally live.

Are there certain things that all plants need to grow?

Yes. In addition to minerals, all plants need a suitable climate, light, moisture, and carbon dioxide. These things are all part of a plant's environment. But hereditary factors also affect a plant's growth.

Hereditary factors? What are they?

Hereditary factors are the characteristics that continue from one generation to the next. A flower's color, for example, or the shape of a leaf is determined by the hereditary factors passed from the parent plant to the new plant.

How do plants manage to grow in places like the desert?

Desert plants have special characteristics that set them apart from most other plants and that allow them to survive in a hot, dry climate. For example, they grow far apart from one another and have root systems that reach out over large areas. This enables each plant to gather enough of the precious soil minerals and water it needs to survive. Cactus plants have large, fleshy stems that store water for the plant to use during long dry spells.

What about plants that grow in water? They have much different needs, don't they?

Yes. Many of them have air spaces in their stems to help hold the plant upright and carry air down to the roots. Some have underwater leaves that are specifically designed to absorb carbon dioxide from water. Certain kinds of algae have something called a *holdfast*, which is a rootlike structure that anchors the plant to rocks and reefs.

How do plants survive in cold areas?

Plants that live on the high mountaintops or in the cold tundra regions near the North Pole pop out only during the brief, cool summers. They grow in low clumps, so they're protected from the cold and wind.

Are there any places where plants can't grow?

Very few. The only places in the world where plants can't grow are places that have a permanent cover of ice. That includes parts of Antarctica, the Arctic, and Greenland. With the exception of those few isolated areas, plants grow everywhere.

Technology:
A modern challenge

What is technology?

Technology is the science of the mechanical and industrial arts. Another way to define technology is to say that it is "applied science," where people use special techniques and tools to achieve a certain goal. Modern society is highly technological. In fact, the age we live in is called the "age of technology," so dependent are we on the industrial sciences.

When did modern society begin?

With the Industrial Revolution, which had its origin in Great Britain in the 1700s. It was then that the development of industry began to take people out of their homes and workshops and place the people in factories to operate machines.

Why did the Industrial Revolution take place?

Generally, it took place because of the invention and development of *power-driven* machinery. These machines manufactured products that before had been made by hand. Also developed at this time were large machines like the steamboat and the steam engine.

What was important about the steam engine?

The key word is *power:* the steam engine had enough power to run the new machines. The old sources of energy such as horses and water wheels did not.

What were a couple of important early industries in Great Britain?

One important one was the textile, or cloth, industry. A spectacular feature of the Industrial Revolution was the introduction of power-driven spinning and weaving machines. These began to make the cloth that people had made at home—by hand—for centuries. The *factory* came into being to house the machines and the people who ran them.

Also, we have the coal and iron industry. Coal was important because it provided the power to drive the ever-present steam engines. Coal was also needed to make iron. Iron was used to improve machines and tools and to build bridges and ships.

So technology was important to the Industrial Revolution?

It was crucial, as it is today. Modern industrial technology develops and uses the discoveries and inventions of scientists to manufacture complicated things: automobiles, medicines, and skyscrapers, for example.

When did airline service begin?

Regularly scheduled airline service in the United States actually began in Florida in 1914. Tony Jannus piloted a flying boat between St. Petersburg and Tampa.

What is an example of how a modern product came from a scientific discovery and invention?

Take electricity. In 1831, Michael Faraday, an English physicist, discovered that as he moved a coil of copper wire near a magnet, he created an electric current in the wire. Thus, Faraday discovered the principle of *electromagnetic induction*. Then, during the late 1800s, Thomas A. Edison invented the electric light. Applying Faraday's discovery and Edison's invention, modern technology was able to bring electric lights to us in our homes in the early 1900s.

Do modern technologists keep track of all the new inventions and discoveries?

They try to; after all, the new inventions and discoveries improve the old products. When James Watt of Scotland began working to improve the steam engine in the 1760s, he could not find a tool that drilled a perfectly round hole. As a result, his engines leaked steam. But in 1775, the operation of the steam engine improved vastly because of the invention of a boring machine that drilled a precise hole.

Technologists usually don't lose track of old inventions and discoveries, either. A good example is Sir Isaac Newton's work in England around 1687. At that time, he provided the scientific knowledge that played a vital part in the invention of jet propulsion engines and rocket engines almost three hundred years later—in our time. It has taken this long for modern technology to develop the engines that could put Newton's scientific knowledge to use.

In what way has technology aided people?

The increased production of goods and services is one major benefit of technology. In farming, manufacturing, mining, and other industries, workers today produce many times more goods than workers did a hundred years ago.

But haven't the machines and factories also polluted our environment?

That is unfortunately true. Environmental pollution ranks as one of the more harmful problems created by technology. Most industrial countries face problems of air, water, soil, and noise pollution. Motor vehicles and many other products and processes of technology cause the polluting. Certain insecticides pollute the soil and water. Factory smoke and wastes pollute the air and water, and these chemicals endanger plant and animal life. Power plants that burn oil to generate electricity add millions of tons of pollutants. And junkyards, open-pit mines, logging operations, and freeways detract from the beauty of the natural environment.

Has technology had more good effects or more bad effects?

Who can say? There's no doubt that pollution in the age of technology is a terrible problem. Add to that the problem of monotonous jobs. In factories some workers have to tend one machine constantly and perform the same task again and again. Work like that can be demanding and unsatisfying.

But technology also has good effects that cannot be ignored. Technology, for example, has decreased the amount of work needed to produce goods and services. In the early 1800s, most factory work was done by hand or hand-operated machines. Workers labored 12 to 16 hours a day, six days a week. Few people ever had a vacation. Today, powered machinery has largely replaced hand labor in factories. As a result, the amount of work-hours needed to produce manufactured goods has decreased sharply. Most factory employees work only 8 hours a day, five days a week. They also receive paid holidays and vacations.

But if less labor is needed, then fewer workers are needed, right?

Yes. A big problem resulting from advances in technology is technological unemployment. This occurs when machines take over workers' jobs. The use of these machines, which is called *automation,* has caused some unemployment. But it has not been so severe as once predicted. And technology has even helped some industries to expand. As a result, these industries have been able to provide new jobs for displaced laborers. But technological unemployment still remains a threat to many workers.

Labor is easier now than it used to be?

Yes, technology has made labor easier—and safer. Take coal mining. In the early 1900s, miners toiled all day with pick and shovel to produce a few tons of coal. The mines were dark, poorly ventilated, and dangerous. Today mining is still dangerous, but better lighting and ventilation and improved safety devices have reduced the hazards. The work itself is easier and more productive because machines perform most of the hard labor.

Will the coal we need for power ever run out?

It could, and that is another minus for technology. It threatens not only the supply of coal but other natural resources such as oil and gas.

The use of electrically powered machinery in the United States and other industrial countries has greatly increased factory production. At the same time, it has reduced the supply of oil and other fuels used to produce electricity. We cannot replace these fuels once we use them up. As power production increases, the supply of fuels decreases. The United States began to experience fuel and power shortages during the 1970s because its power production increased so greatly during the 1950s and after.

With so many disadvantages, why do many countries continue to be industrial nations?

We can point to the high living standards of the peoples of the industrial nations for your answer. Increased production of goods and services means that most people are better fed, clothed, and housed. And they enjoy a healthier, more comfortable life than any other people in history.

What are some of the technological goods that make a more comfortable life?

Let's take the products from just one area: the manufacturing industry. It provides us with packaged food products that are quick and easy to cook. Also, it gives us cars, buses, and airplanes. Don't forget our modern medicines—all of these are manufactured. And look at the printed matter available to us: books, magazines, newspapers. These are manufactured products, too.

Are there different steps in manufacturing different products?

The steps in the manufacturing industry are the same for nearly all types of products, from clothing to computers. First the manufacturer designs the product. Then, he buys the raw materials needed to make it. Workers at the factory use the raw materials to produce the finished product. After workers complete the product, a salesman sells it to customers.

What is another important industry besides manufacturing?

Agriculture. In fact, it is our most important one. Agriculture provides us with almost all our food. It also supplies materials for two other basic human needs: clothing and shelter. In addition, agriculture provides materials used in making many industrial products such as paints and medicines. And about half the world's workers are employed in agriculture—far more than in any other industry.

What are the farmers' food products?

The main group is cereal grains such as barley, corn, millet, oats, rice, rye, sorghum, and wheat. The second important group is root crops, a basic food for many people. Root crops include potatoes, sweet potatoes, and a tropical plant called cassava. The six remaining groups of major food crops are (1) pulses, which consist mainly of dry beans and peas; (2) fruits and vegetables other than root crops and pulses; (3) oil-bearing crops such as soybeans and coconuts; (4) sugar-bearing crops, especially sugar cane and sugar beets; (5) nuts; and (6) cocoa beans, coffee, and tea.

As for animals raised for food, familiar examples are cattle, chickens, goats, hogs, and sheep. Every country raises livestock, which supply nearly all the world's meat, eggs, and milk. Some farmers keep bees for honey, and some raise freshwater fish on fish farms.

	1850	Today

How much has traveling speed increased since we've had modern transportation?

Since 1850, overland transportation speed has increased from 9 mph (14 kph) to 130 mph (209 kph). Water transportation has gone from 23 mph (37 kph) to 75 mph (121 kph). Air transportation did not exist in 1850, but in 1852 Henri Giffard, a French engineer, drove his cigar-shaped balloon about 5 mph (8 kph). Modern air transportation can carry travelers at 600 mph (965 kph).

What are some non-food farm products?

Natural fibers, which come from a variety of plants
and animals raised on farms. Mills and factories use
cotton, flax, hemp, jute, sisal, and wool in textile
products. Silk fibers are obtained from the cocoons of
silkworms raised mostly in Japan and China.

Many farms provide other raw materials for industry
besides fibers. These include natural rubber, animal
hides, and vegetable oils such as castor oil and
linseed oil. These are used in paints and medicines.

If farmers are so productive in the age of technology, why are some nations short of food?

Since the early 1950s, the demand for food throughout the world has more than doubled. The primary
cause for the staggering new demand is increase in
population. In the "developing" countries—the poor-
er nations—population growth has overwhelmed the
already small food production.

What have farmers done about the tremendous need for food?

In North America, they have expanded their output
enormously. There has also been a large growth in
agricultural trade among nations. From the late 1960s
to the mid-1970s, the total world trade in farm
products more than doubled.

What can the developing nations do to increase their own food production?

Well, these countries are encouraged to expand their
own food production greatly in order to avert a
desperate food shortage. But the developing nations
need help in getting farming programs going.

Will the developing countries use technology to increase their food production?

Yes, but they cannot put technology into effect as easily as can the industrial nations. Developing countries lack the resources that scientific farming requires. They receive help from programs provided by many countries and by the Food and Agriculture Organization, an agency of the United Nations. As a result of these various efforts, the developing countries did double their food production during the 1960s. But much remains to be done to solve the world's food-supply problems.

You've mentioned farming, mining, and manufacturing. These industries all go way back into history. Aren't there any brand-new industries?

Of course. The newest of all is the computer industry.

How do computers help us?

Computers have enormously expanded the amount of work people and machines can do. At the same time, there is a tremendous increase in the amount of scientific research that can be conducted—in all fields—as a result of computer development.

Who invented the computer?

Several inventors combined many ideas and devices to produce the electronic computer. In the 1830s, Charles Babbage, an English mathematician, developed the idea of a mechanical digital computer—one that solves problems by counting numbers, like a cash register. Babbage never made a machine, but computers today are based on many of the principles used in Babbage's design.

In 1930, Vannevar Bush, an American electrical engineer, built the first analog computer. This computer measures one quantity in terms of another. Think of this computer as if it were a thermometer. A thermometer indicates temperature—one quantity—in terms of another: a thin line of liquid. The line becomes longer as the temperature varies. The same principle applies to analog computers.

World War II (1939–45) saw the development of both analog and digital computers. By the 1950s, the manufacture of computers had become an industry.

Computers can't operate on their own, can they?

No, but they are so "smart," we call them "electronic brains." Human operators must put facts and figures into the computer and then tell the computer what to do with the information. But a computer has a "memory" that stores the information. And there is another unit in a computer that performs mathematical operations. This unit is called an *arthmetic*. It's pronounced AR *ihth* MEHT *ihk*.

What industries can use computers?

Almost all industries can use them. Some companies have computers for bookkeeping and accounting. Engineers use computers to check the design of buildings, bridges, and dams. Astronauts keep their spaceships on course with computers, and newspaper and book publishers set type with them.

In other industries, computers control machines that make products. A computer turns the machines on and off, adjusting their operation when necessary. Machinery controlled by computers is used in making bakery goods, chemicals, steel products, paper, and many other items.

Modern farm machines have helped produce larger crops. But just how much more food can each farmer produce with modern technology?

In 1850 a farmer in the United States could produce enough food for 4 persons. Today, a U.S. farmer produces roughly fourteen times that amount: enough food for about 56 persons.

What will the computers of the future be like?

They will operate more and more as parts of "networks": groups of several computers linked by communications lines. Network computers exchange data directly among one another. A network might also include terminals in banks, department stores, and homes.

Does computer technology create some problems, as other technologies do?

Well, computers collect facts in *data banks*. As these banks grow, businesses and government collect more and more personal and business information, information that can make people lose more and more of their privacy. Various groups, including legislators and computer designers, are working to prevent the unauthorized use of information in data banks.

Then computer technology has its own problem to solve?

Yes, and the chief challenge in this technology—and all technologies—is to combat the undesirable and sometimes quite unexpected side effects resulting from technological development. The automobile makers can work to curb air pollution by trying to find a means of purifying auto exhausts. Other manufacturers can help to conserve mineral and timber resources by the process of recycling waste products. And the computer industry can work to insure the privacy of the individual.

United States —
its people and places

How big is the United States in area?

The United States covers more than 3.5 million square miles (9 million square kilometers), not including coastal water, Lake St. Clair, and the Great Lakes.

Is the United States the largest country in the world?

No. It ranks fourth in both area and population.

How big are the Great Lakes?

The Great Lakes—the largest group of freshwater lakes in the world—have a total area in the United States of 60,590 square miles (156,927 square kilometers), nearly the combined area of Connecticut, Maine, Massachusetts, New Hampshire, Rhode Island, and Vermont.

What are the smallest and largest states in area?

Rhode Island is the smallest of the 50 states, and Alaska is by far the largest. Alaska has almost one-fifth of the total U.S. area.

Does Alaska have a big population, too?

No. In fact, Alaska has the smallest population of any of the 50 states.

Which state has the largest population?

California ranks first in population.

How far is Alaska from the rest of the U.S. mainland?

Alaska is about 500 miles (800 kilometers) north of the rest of the U.S. mainland.

Isn't Alaska the northernmost part of the country?

Yes. Point Barrow, Alaska, is the northernmost point in the entire United States. Alaska also has the westernmost point—Cape Wrangell, on Attu Island. Alaska's far northwestern location brings U.S. territory close to Russia.

How can that be? Isn't Russia far away from the United States?

Russia is far from the 48 mainland states and Hawaii. But the westernmost part of the Alaskan mainland is only 51 miles (82 kilometers) from Russia. And Alaska's Little Diomede Island lies only about 2.5 miles (4 kilometers) from Russia's Big Diomede Island.

What's the easternmost point in the United States?

West Quoddy Head, Maine, is the easternmost point.

Does Florida have the southernmost point?

Florida has the southernmost point only on the U.S. mainland. Ka Lae, Hawaii, is the southernmost point in the entire country.

How many islands make up Hawaii?

Hawaii has a total of 132 islands, 8 of which we consider major islands.

Do people live on all the islands?

No. People live on only seven of the eight major islands. The minor islands are much too small for people to live on. They are tiny volcanic islands with a combined area of only 3 square miles (8 square kilometers).

Does Hawaii have many volcanoes?

Yes, but most of them are inactive. Alaska has almost all the active volcanoes in the United States. It also has the country's 14 highest mountains.

What's the highest mountain in the United States?

Mount McKinley in Alaska is the highest. It rises 20,320 feet (6,194 meters) above sea level.

What's the lowest point in the United States?

The lowest is Death Valley, in California. It lies 282 feet (86 meters) below sea level in the Great Basin.

Are there any bodies of water in the Great Basin?

This desert region has many saltwater lakes, the largest of which is the Great Salt Lake in Utah.

Are the salt lakes as salty as the ocean?

They're actually much saltier than the ocean. The high salt content of the Great Salt Lake, for example, makes it just about impossible for a swimmer to sink.

Are there freshwater rivers or lakes in the Great Basin?

There are riverbeds and flat areas that fill up with water during rainstorms, but they dry up afterward.

Does the region receive much rainfall?

No, the region as a whole is quite dry. And Death Valley in particular is the driest—and the hottest—place in the entire United States.

How much rainfall does Death Valley get?

The average annual rainfall in Death Valley is less than 2 inches (5 centimeters).

How does that compare with the wettest place in the United States?

The wettest place—Mount Waialeale on Kauai Island in Hawaii—gets an average of 460 inches (1,170 centimeters) of rainfall a year.

What's the hottest temperature ever recorded at Death Valley?

Death Valley set a U.S. record in 1913, when the temperature there reached 134° F (57° C).

What was the lowest temperature in U.S. history?

The lowest temperature was −80° F (−62° C), recorded at Prospect Creek, Alaska, in 1971.

Is it always cold in Alaska?

Much of Alaska has warm summers. The state has even recorded temperatures as high as 100° F (38° C).

Then can crops grow in Alaska? Are there farms there?

There are many farms in Alaska. Two-thirds of Alaska lies below the Arctic Circle. The soil and climate in that part of the state are suitable for growing crops and raising livestock. In fact, crops grow quickly because the sun shines for about 20 hours a day during Alaska's summers.

What U.S. state ranks first in agriculture?

California leads the nation in the total value of its agricultural production. It produces more artichokes, brussels sprouts, asparagus, broccoli, carrots, cauliflower, celery, lettuce, tomatoes, grapes, and eggs than any other state.

Do most Californians live on farms?

No. In fact, only 9% of the people in California live in rural areas, which include farms and towns with fewer than 2,500 people.

Which state has the highest percentage of rural dwellers?

Vermont. About 70% of Vermont's population live in rural areas.

What's the largest city in the United States?

New York City is the largest city in population. It also ranks as the fifth largest city in the world, after Shanghai, Mexico City, Tokyo, and Peking. Only six states, not including New York State, have populations larger than New York City.

Is New York City the largest U.S. city in area, too?

No. Juneau, Alaska, is the largest in area. But it has a relatively small population. Juneau—like the rest of Alaska—has a low population density, meaning it has few people per acre or other land unit. Alaska has the lowest population density of all the states.

What state among the 48 mainland states has the lowest density?

That would be Wyoming. And New Jersey has the highest.

What is the largest U.S. minority group?

Blacks make up the largest minority group, followed by Mexican Americans.

Which state has the largest black population?

New York has the largest black population of all the states. And New York City has more blacks than any other city in the world.

Which state has the largest Mexican-American population?

California and Texas have the largest Mexican-American populations. Los Angeles has more persons of Mexican ancestry than any other urban area outside Mexico.

How about the American Indians? What percentage of the U.S. population are they?

American Indians make up less than .5% of the U.S. population.

Which state has the largest number of Indians?

Oklahoma has more Indians than any other state. The name *Oklahoma* comes from two Choctaw Indian words meaning "red people."

Do most of the Indians live on reservations?

About half of them do.

How many reservations are there?

There are about 285 reservations. They cover large portions of some states. About a fourth of the area of Arizona, for example, is reservation land.

The Indians were the first Americans, weren't they?

Yes. The Indians were the first people to live on what is now the United States mainland. They migrated to America from Asia thousands of years ago. All Americans, including the Indians, are immigrants or the descendants of immigrants. The United States has received more immigrants than any other nation.

How much do companies spend on advertising in the United States each year?

Each year in the United States, companies spend more than $33 billion on advertising. Of that, 30% goes to newspaper advertising; 19.7% to television; 14.1% to direct mail; 6.8% to radio; and 5.3% to magazines. That's roughly 75% of the money spent. The rest goes to business publications, outdoor signs, farm publications and other advertising (McCann-Erickson, Inc.).

From what countries did the larger groups of non-Indian immigrants come?

Most of the early American colonists came to the East Coast from England. Later, the largest number of European immigrants to that area came from Germany, Italy, and Ireland. And most American blacks are descendants of slaves brought to this country from Africa.

Is the oldest U.S. city in New England?

No, the oldest U.S. city is St. Augustine, Florida, in the South. The Spanish founded St. Augustine in 1565. But probably the oldest continuously settled place in the entire country is a Hopi Indian settlement at Oraibi, Arizona. The Hopis built Oraibi in the 1100s.

What was the first English settlement in America?

The colonists established the first English settlement in America in 1585 on Roanoke Island, off the coast of what is now North Carolina. But the settlement failed. The first successful English settlement was Jamestown, Virginia, established in 1607. Virginia thus became the first of the 13 colonies.

Were the other 12 colonies formed at about the same time?

It took over 100 years to form the other 12 colonies. The settlement period lasted from 1620, when the Pilgrims landed at Plymouth, in Massachusetts, to 1733, when Georgia colonized.

Which colony was the first to declare its independence from Britain?

New Hampshire was the first. It adopted its own constitution on January 5, 1776. But we recognize July 4, 1776, as Independence Day. With 12 colonies voting, the Continental Congress approved the Declaration of Independence on that day. New York did not approve until July 9. July 4 is also the anniversary of the deaths of three U.S. Presidents.

Which three Presidents died on July 4?

John Adams and Thomas Jefferson died on the same day in the same year: July 4, 1826. This was exactly 50 years after the adoption of the Declaration of Independence. James Monroe died on July 4, 1831.

How many Presidents died while in office?

Eight Presidents died in office. They are William Henry Harrison, Zachary Taylor, Abraham Lincoln, James Garfield, William McKinley, Warren Harding, Franklin Roosevelt, and John Kennedy. Harrison served as President only one month—the shortest term of any President.

Who served the longest term?

Franklin Roosevelt. He served for 12 years, 1 month, and 8 days.

Did any President marry in the White House?

Only Grover Cleveland, who in 1886 married Frances Folsom in the Blue Room. Folsom was 21 and Cleveland was 49. The bride was the youngest First Lady in U.S. history and became the mother of Esther Cleveland, the only President's child born in the White House.

Cleveland called Frances by her nickname, "Frank."

Has Washington, D.C., always been the U.S. capital?

No. Washington didn't become the capital until 1800. At various times before that, Congress met in Philadelphia; Baltimore; Lancaster, Pennsylvania; York, Pennsylvania; Princeton, New Jersey; Annapolis, Maryland; Trenton, New Jersey; and New York City.

Who was the first President to be inaugurated in Washington?

Thomas Jefferson.

Was Jefferson the first President to live in the White House?

No. John Adams was the first President to live in the White House. He was in office when the government moved to Washington. Jefferson became President after Adams.

When was the Constitution written and adopted?

The Constitution was written in 1787. Delaware became the first state to approve the Constitution, and the document was officially adopted when New Hampshire ratified it on June 21, 1788. The U.S. Constitution is the oldest of all written national constitutions presently in use.

Has the Constitution changed much over the years?

Not really. Congress has considered more than 7,000 amendments to the Constitution. But it has approved only 32, and only 26 amendments have been ratified.

When did U.S. territory include all the land that the 48 mainland states now occupy?

The general boundaries of the mainland United States were complete by 1854. But at that time, there were only 31 states. The rest of the land was divided into various territories or was unorganized. In 1912, when Arizona and New Mexico joined the Union, the division of the mainland into 48 states was complete.

When did Alaska and Hawaii become states?

In 1959, Alaska and Hawaii became the forty-ninth and fiftieth states.

How did the United States gain control of Alaska?

In 1867, the U.S. Secretary of State, William H. Seward, bought Alaska from Russia for $7,200,000.

Wasn't that a lot of money to pay?

Many people thought so and criticized the purchase as "Seward's Folly." But, in fact, the land cost the United States only about 2 cents an acre (5 cents a hectare). The huge mineral and other resources later discovered in Alaska made the purchase one of the great bargains in U.S. history.

The United States as a whole is rich in natural resources, isn't it?

Yes, indeed. Forests cover about a third of the United States, and farmland for crops and grazing comprises about half the land. The nation's mineral resources are also huge.

What are some of the leading agricultural states?

California leads the nation in vegetable production, Illinois ranks first in soybeans, and Iowa is first in corn. Kansas leads in wheat, and Texas is first in cotton.

Which states are leading cattle producers?

Wisconsin has more dairy cattle than any other state, and Texas ranks first in beef cattle.

How does the United States rank among the nations of the world in its mineral production?

The United States is a leading producer of important minerals such as petroleum, coal, and iron ore. And it produces more natural gas and copper than any other nation in the world.

Which states produce the most oil, gas, and coal?

Texas and Louisiana are the leaders in oil and natural gas production. Kentucky, West Virginia, and Pennsylvania are the leading coal producers. Oil, coal, and gas are the source of almost all the nation's energy.

Does the United States produce enough of these fuels to supply all its energy needs?

No. Although the United States produces enough coal to export to other nations, it imports huge amounts of oil to meet its energy requirements.

Why do we have to import so much oil?

There are various reasons. But one of the more important is that, per person, Americans use about six times more energy than persons in any other country.

With only about 5% of the world's population, the United States uses about 30% of the world's energy.

Which U.S. states are leading suppliers of chief metals?

About four-fifths of the country's iron ore comes from Michigan, Wisconsin, and Minnesota. Arkansas has about 90% of the U.S. supply of bauxite, the ore used in making aluminum. Wyoming is first in uranium, and Arizona has more than half of U.S. copper. Idaho ranks first in silver, and South Dakota produces more gold than any other state.

Did the first U.S. gold rush take place in South Dakota?

No, the first gold rush in the United States took place around Dahlonega, Georgia, in 1828. But gold mining ended there in 1849 after the discovery of gold in California attracted thousands of fortune hunters.

Does the United States have any diamond fields?

The only diamond field in all of North America is in Murfreesboro, Arkansas. Most diamonds mined in that field have not been of great commercial value, but one was worth $250,000.

Is the United States a leading manufacturing nation?

The United States ranks first among all nations in the value of its manufactured products. There are almost 320,000 manufacturing plants in the United States. They produce about a fourth of the world's manufactured goods.

1850

Today

There is so much manufacturing in the United States. Who does all the work?

A better question would be *what* does all the work. Today, machines do over 98% of the work in the United States. People do only 1%, and animals do less than 1%. Compare those figures with the ones for 1850. Then, machines did 35% of the work, people did 13%, and animals did the most work of all: 52%.

What's the most valuable manufactured product?

Nonelectric machinery is first, with transportation equipment—mainly cars and trucks—ranking second. The United States produces more cars than any other country.

Which states lead in manufacturing?

California, New York, and Ohio lead. The value of products manufactured in New York alone is about 8% of the U.S. total. New York also leads the nation in the value of its foreign trade.

What country is the United States' most important trade partner?

Canada is by far its most important trade partner. Canada receives about a fifth of all U.S. exports and is the source of about a fifth of U.S. imports.

How does the United States transport most of its imports and exports?

Ships carry most U.S. international trade goods. In tonnage, the U.S. merchant fleet is the seventh largest in the world.

What is the country's largest seaport?

By tonnage handled, New York City is the biggest.

How does the United States transport most goods within the states?

Railroads are the major freight carriers in the United States. But for passenger transportation, automobiles and airlines lead the railroads.

What's the biggest airport in the United States?

The biggest in area is the Dallas-Fort Worth Airport.
But the busiest in the country—and the world—is
Chicago-O'Hare International Airport.

How many automobiles are there in the United States?

There are more than 100 million cars registered in the
United States. That's nearly half the world total.
Americans everywhere use cars to get to and from
work and to travel to the nation's vacation spots.

What kinds of places rank among the leading U.S. tourist attractions?

The United States has a tremendous number and
variety of attractions in its cities and countryside.
Many of the more popular are part of the National
Park System, which includes nearly 300 parks, monu-
ments, historic sites, memorials, recreation areas,
battlefields, and national lakeshores and seashores.
Every state except Delaware has at least one national
parkland.

What's the largest national park?

Yellowstone National Park in Wyoming is the largest.
Established in 1872, it's also the oldest.

What are some of the national monuments that are part of the park system?

One of the more famous is the Statue of Liberty in
New York—one of the larger statues in the world. The
monument at Fort Sumter, South Carolina, marks the
site of the start of the U.S. Civil War.

What are some of the more scenic areas included in the park system?

Some of the more spectacular natural wonders include the huge underground caves of Carlsbad Caverns in New Mexico, the dunes and beaches of the Cape Cod National Seashore in Massachusetts, and the breathtaking gorges of the Grand Canyon in Arizona. Add to these the giant redwood and sequoia trees of California; the mountain rain forests in the state of Washington; and the glaciers, lakes, and mountains of Alaska. In the South, there are the forested Blue Ridge Mountains of Virginia and the subtropical wilderness of the Florida Everglades.

How many visitors go each year to places in the National Park System?

There are more than 260 million visitors each year, and the number steadily increases. More and more people come to national parklands to learn about U.S. history and simply to enjoy the incredible beauty of the many natural wonders that lie within the boundaries of the United States.

Canada, land of beauty and progress

Is Canada as large as it looks on the map?

Canada is the second largest country in the world. Only Russia has more land. Canada is about 176,000 square miles (455,800 square kilometers) larger than the United States. But only about a tenth as many people live in Canada as in its southern neighbor. The estimated 1979 population of Canada is 23,901,000 persons. Compare that to the estimated 1979 population of the United States: 220,806,000.

Where in Canada do most Canadians live?

Most live within 200 miles (320 kilometers) of their southern border. This is because much of northern Canada is a wilderness of forest and frozen wasteland. The number of Canadians living in this 200-mile strip—which is the common United States/Canadian border—means that the populations of the two countries live rather close to each other. The common border of the United States and Canada is 3,987 miles (6,416 kilometers) long.

Since Canada and the United States are such close neighbors, do they ever cooperate to the benefit of both countries?

Yes. Common interests and a common background have created a bond of friendship between Canadians and Americans. Through the North American Air Defense Command, they stand guard together against any possible air attack. Both Canadian and United States military personnel operate radar stations that serve both nations. There is also cooperation in matters of weather. Meteorologists—scientists who study weather—send weather reports south by radio from isolated stations in the Arctic.

Is Canada an exciting land to visit?

It is rich in scenic beauty and natural resources. Colorful fishing villages hug the foggy Atlantic coast. The glow from factories and mills lights the night sky above busy industrial centers. There are rushing rivers and plunging waterfalls. Golden wheat fields cover western province plains. The thriving farms offer a vivid contrast to Canada's ice-covered islands in the Arctic Ocean. The far west—with its towering, snow-capped mountains, deep green valleys, and sparkling lakes—is one of the world's more scenic regions.

Where does the word *Canada* come from?

It is from the Iroquoian Indian word *Kanata* or *Kanada*, which means "village" or "group of huts."

Eskimos live in Canada, don't they?

Eskimos live in the Canadian Arctic Islands. Scattered groups of Eskimos there support themselves by fishing and hunting. There are also fur traders, missionaries, and meteorologists in the Arctic. They live in small, isolated trading posts along the coasts of the islands.

Do the people of Canada speak several languages?

Yes. Canada has two official languages: English and French. Almost all Canadians trace their ancestry to Europeans. About 45 of every 100 are of British descent. About 30 of every 100 are the descendants of early French settlers. So, both French and English appear on postage stamps and money. Both languages are also used in debates in the Canadian parliament.

The languages other than French and English are those spoken by the Eskimos and Indians. There are more than 295,000 Indians and about 17,500 Eskimos in the country's population.

Is Canada an agricultural country?

It was in the early 1900s. But today, Canada ranks among the 10 leading industrial nations in the world.

Then the more important activity is industry, not farming?

Yes. The manufacturing industry, for example, accounts for over two-thirds of the value of all goods produced in Canada.

Is Canada also a trading country?

One of the leading ones. Its imports and exports total

over $65 billion each year. Canada exports about half the goods it produces, and imports about half the goods it uses.

Is mining important in Canada?

Canada leads the world in the production of asbestos, silver, nickel, and zinc. It ranks second in the mining of copper, gypsum, and potash. And it is a leading producer of cadmium, cobalt, gold, iron ore, lead, magnesium, molybdenum, natural gas, platinum, sulfur, titanium, and uranium. But petroleum—called black gold because of its value—is Canada's most valuable mining product.

Did Canada ever have a great oil strike?

In 1947 there was a great oil strike at Leduc in the province of Alberta. Annual petroleum production jumped from about 8 million barrels in that year to a peak of about 650 million barrels in the mid-1970s.

Where are the fertile lands in Canada?

Much rich black soil is found in the Prairie Provinces. Wheat, barley, oats, rapeseed, rye, hay, clover, sugar beets, cattle, and hogs come from these provinces. In net value, farmers there and in other parts of Canada produce almost $8.9 billion worth of farm products, or 15% of the value of all goods produced in the country. The gray-brown soil of the St. Lawrence-Great Lakes Lowlands is also good for farming.

Does Canada have any very old industries?

Canada has industries that go back to colonial times, and before. Take fishing. Canada is one of the top fishing countries in the world. The value of its annual catch is about $290 million, or 1,000,000 short tons (900,000 metric tons) of fish and other seafood. The Atlantic Ocean gives up cod, flounder, haddock, herring, redfish, sole, lobsters, crabs, scallops, and tuna. Glistening salmon caught near mouths of rivers are the most important product of the Pacific coast. Other seafood caught in the Pacific Ocean are cod, crabs, halibut, herring, and sole. Fish from the lakes and rivers—herring, perch, pickerel, sauger, smelt, and whitefish—provide fresh catches for inland Canada and the United States.

What is the Canadian Shield?

The Canadian Shield is a great, horseshoe-shaped region that covers almost half of Canada. The Shield curves around Hudson Bay from the Arctic shore of the Northwest Territories to the northern coast of Quebec. The eastern part of the region forms the great Laurentian Uplands north of the St. Lawrence River. Hills dot the rock surface of the Canadian Shield.

The Shield is known as a vast treasure house. It is made up of ancient and extremely hard rocks. Underneath the surface are numerous minerals, including copper, gold, iron, lead, nickel, platinum, silver, uranium, and zinc.

How about the other land regions of Canada?

Canada has an amazing variety of land regions, with everything except desert and jungle. The six regions in addition to the Canadian Shield are:
1. *The Appalachian Region.* This forms part of the ancient Appalachian Mountain system, extending from the state of Alabama, in the United States, to the province of Newfoundland, in Canada.

2. *The St. Lawrence-Great Lakes Lowlands*. About half the population lives in this region. Industry and farming thrive here.

3. *The Hudson Bay Lowland*. This is a low, wet, rocky plain wedged between the Canadian Shield and the southwestern coast of Hudson Bay. Swamps and low forests cover most of this thinly populated region.

4. *The Western Interior Plains region*. Here we find the Canadian section of the Great Plains of North America. It spreads northward to the Arctic Ocean. Besides the great prairies, where farmers raise wheat, the region is loaded with deposits of coal, petroleum, potash, and natural gas.

5. *The Western Mountain Region*, or the *Cordilleran Region*. The rugged front range of the Canadian Rockies forms the eastern boundary of this area. Mount Robson, the highest peak in the Canadian Rockies, towers 12,972 feet (3,954 meters) above sea level in eastern British Columbia. A long, narrow valley called Rocky Mountain Trench is west of the Rockies. West of the trench are plateaus, deep valleys, basins, and low mountains. The Coast Mountains rise along the Pacific Ocean, extending to the Yukon Territory. Another mountain range, partially covered by the Pacific Ocean, forms Vancouver Island and the Queen Charlotte Islands.

6. *The Arctic Islands*. These lie almost entirely within the Arctic Circle.

How about Canada's coastline?

It is one of the longest coastlines of any country. Including island coasts, Canada's coastline extends 151,489 miles (243,798 kilometers). It extends along the Atlantic, Arctic, and Pacific oceans, and along Hudson Bay, Hudson Strait, and James Bay. The Great Lakes shoreline alone is 4,726 miles (7,606 kilometers). The Arctic coast stretches 68,900 miles

(110,884 kilometers)—almost half of the total coast-line.

Did the pioneers use the St. Lawrence River system and the Great Lakes to settle Canada?

Yes. These served as routes inland for colonists from Europe. The St. Lawrence River was sometimes called the "Mother of Canada." With the Great Lakes, today it forms a great water highway in North America.

How does the St. Lawrence Seaway fit into this great water highway?

For a long time, Canada and the United States wanted to make it possible for the large oceangoing ships to sail directly from the Atlantic Ocean to ports like Chicago and even as far west as ports on Lake Superior. There was a need for locks and canals to carry the large ships between the narrow and shallow parts of the St. Lawrence waterway. The United States and Canada jointly built these locks and canals. Queen Elizabeth II and President Dwight D. Eisenhower officially opened the St. Lawrence Sea-way in June 1959.

Is the St. Lawrence Seaway effective?

Highly effective. In the mid-1970s, for example, ships on the seaway annually carried about 54 million short tons (49 million metric tons) of cargo. This is almost five times what the old canals carried. The chief North American products shipped on the seaway have become iron ore from Minnesota and Labrador and grains from the Midwest. Foreign cargo includes automobiles and heavy machinery.

Canada has such huge forests. Do Canadians manufacture lots of paper from the trees?

Certainly. Canada's enormous forests actually provide the world's greatest supply of newsprint. Canada is one of the world's leading wood-producing countries, too. Half of this wood comes from one province: British Columbia. Logs from Canadian forests are sent to mills that make them into paper, lumber, plywood, and wood pulp.

Do the Great Lakes split the United States and Canada?

Not quite. Lake Michigan lies entirely within the United States. But the border between the United States and Canada passes through the other four Great Lakes and the rivers that connect them.

Are there any spectacular sights on the Great Lakes?

There's Niagara Falls. The Niagara River forms the falls as it plunges over a great rock ledge. The river flows between and joins Lakes Ontario and Erie.

Niagara Falls is known throughout America as a honeymooners' paradise. The Falls also provide one of the greatest natural sources of water power in North America. Hydroelectric plants there supply electricity to homes and industries throughout the province of Ontario, as well as in the states of New York and Pennsylvania.

How large are Canada's forests?

Enormous. Canadian forests cover about 1,300,000 square miles (3,400,000 square kilometers), or about a third of Canada's land area. The western forest runs from the mountain ranges of Alberta to the coastal area of British Columbia. The southeastern forest covers parts of Ontario, Quebec, and the Atlantic provinces of Newfoundland, Nova Scotia, and New Brunswick. The northern forest stretches in an unbroken belt across northern Canada from the Atlantic coast to Alaska.

Do many birds fly north to Canada for the summer?

Yes. And Canada is considered a haven for certain U.S. birds threatened with extinction. Two examples of Canada's fair-weather inhabitants are the bald eagle and the golden eagle. Both of these nest in Canada during the summer.

Are there many Canadian fur trappers still in business?

The fur trade has declined since it was the chief source of Canadian wealth in the 1600s and 1700s. But fur trappers still catch animals in some northern regions. The most valuable are beaver, fox, lynx, muskrat, and seal. These account for three-fifths of Canada's fur production. Most animals raised on fur farms are minks.

Have there been gold rushes in Canada as there have been in the United States?

In the 1890s, a gold rush took place in the Klondike. Many prospectors arrived there via the great Yukon River, which rises near the gold fields in the western Yukon Territory. Then it flows westward into Alaska. There is a national park that commemorates the Klondike gold rush of 1897 and 1898. Called the Klondike Gold Rush International Historic Park, the park has sites at Bonanza Creek, Dawson, Lake Bennett, and Whitehorse. The Klondike still produces gold today, worth about $2 million a year.

How was law and order kept in the Canadian west during the early days of settlement?

The "Mounties" saw to Canadian law and order. The North-West Mounted Police was established in 1873 to eliminate illegal trade in whiskey, to collect customs duties, to calm growing unrest among Canadian Indians, and to fight lawlessness. Today, the Royal Mounted Police enforces federal law in Canada.

I've heard there's something called "Fish Ladder" in New Brunswick. What is it?

Fish Ladder, which stands beside the falls in St. George, helps fish to swim upstream so that they can spawn, or produce eggs. New Brunswick has many waterfalls that make upstream traveling difficult for the fish.

Does the Royal Canadian Mounted Police still use horses?

Yes, but only for ceremonies. The force today maintains over 4,500 land motor vehicles, including cars, trucks, and snowmobiles. It has police dogs, too, and air and marine services.

Why are the official uniforms of the Royal Canadian Mounted Police the color scarlet?

The organizers chose scarlet because Indians considered it a symbol of justice and fair dealing. The Indians respected the British soldiers who came to Canada's western plains long before the Mounties came into being, and these early soldiers wore scarlet coats. So, the Mounted Police also chose scarlet. Today they wear it for ceremonies, to carry on the tradition.

Is the government of Canada similar to that of the United States?

Like the United States, Canada is an independent, self-governing democracy. It is also similar in its federal form of government. Canada does, however, combine with the federal form a cabinet system that is like Great Britain's.

Who is the Canadian head of state?

A prime minister directs the Canadian government. But Canada is a member of the Commonwealth of Nations, made up of Great Britain and a group of its former colonies. For this reason, Queen Elizabeth II of England is Canada's symbolic, formal head of state.

The early history of Canada and the United States is similar, isn't it?

Yes. Both countries are nations carved out of a wilderness. Indian tribes occupied both countries before the explorers came. In Canada, there were also scattered tribes of Eskimos. Following the explorers, fur trappers, and missionaries came the people who settled the two countries. Both countries eventually became colonies of Great Britain, and both eventually gained independence from Great Britain.

Did Canada gain its independence from Great Britain in the same way that the United States did—by revolution?

No. The British, acting with insight provided by the American Revolution, gave the Canadian colonists limited self-government in 1848. Because of this, the Canadians remained tied politically to Great Britain for many years afterward. But the trend towards independence was inevitable. In 1931, the British Parliament made the Dominion of Canada an independent country.

Does Canada have a senate?

Yes, but it is not the same as the Senate of the United States, whose members are elected by popular vote. The governor general appoints the Canadian senators on recommendation of the prime minister. The Canadian Senate also has less power than the Canadian House of Commons.

How long does the prime minister remain in office?

Only so long as the prime minister has the backing of the majority of the House of Commons. Without this backing, the prime minister must either resign or appeal for the support of the people in a general election.

Do voting requirements differ in Canada and the United States?

They are quite similar. In Canada, to vote in national elections, a person must be at least 18 years old and a Canadian citizen. Voting requirements vary for elections within the 10 provinces. In the United States, the voting age for both national elections and state elections is 18, and, as in Canada, the person voting must be a citizen of the nation.

Do Canada's future problems resemble those of the United States?

In the future, Canada and the United States face some of the same sorts of problems. One difficulty is unemployment. Another is inflation. Both countries must solve energy problems, and economic downturns trouble Canada and the United States. The two nations seem to share economic dilemmas as well as their historical and cultural backgrounds. It is possible that the future holds yet more similarities in store for them.

A world of nations

What is the biggest country in the world?

Russia.

Is it much larger than the United States?

Russia is larger than the United States and Canada combined. It covers more than 8.5 million square miles (22 million square kilometers), or about a seventh of the world's total land area.

Does Russia have more people than any other country?

No. It ranks third in population, after China and India.

China has a tremendous population, doesn't it?

China has more than 865 million persons. That's more than three times the population of Russia and nearly four times the population of the United States. About one out of five persons in the world lives in China.

Isn't India pretty crowded, too?

India has about 650 million persons. The combined populations of India and China account for more than 35% of the people in the world. Each of those two nations individually has a larger population than North and South America combined.

Are the populations of all countries growing larger?

No. Some countries—East Germany, for example— have a decreasing population. The countries of Latin America, on the other hand, have a rapid rate of population growth. Mexico has one of the highest growth rates. Its population increases by about 3.5% a year.

What's the smallest country in the world?

Vatican City, the administrative headquarters of the Roman Catholic Church, is the smallest. It lies completely within the city limits of Rome and covers only .17 square mile (.44 square kilometer).

Isn't that smaller than most cities, even towns?

Yes. In fact, Vatican City, plus the four other smallest European nations—Monaco, Malta, San Marino, and Liechtenstein—could *all* fit within the city limits of Dallas, Texas.

What's the population of Vatican City?

It has only about 1,000 persons. But because of its small area, it has one of the highest population densities of any country.

Population density? What's that?

Population density is the average number of persons that live in a square mile or square kilometer of land.

Doesn't population density vary a lot within a country?

Yes. The average population density in China as a whole, for example, is about 236 persons per square mile (91 persons per square kilometer). But in some of China's larger urban areas, the density is more than 10 times greater. In other parts of China, there are no people at all.

What are some countries with low population densities?

Saudi Arabia is one. It has only about 10 persons per square mile (4 persons per square kilometer). Botswana, in southern Africa, has only 3 persons per square mile (1 person per square kilometer).

What are some countries with high densities?

A number of European and Asian nations have high population densities. Belgium and The Netherlands both have more than 800 persons per square mile (310 persons per square kilometer). The South Asian nation of Bangladesh has about 1,500 persons per square mile (580 persons per square kilometer).

Is it true that kangaroos live only in Australia?

Only in Australia can we find kangaroos and many other unusual animals. A marsupial, the kangaroo is interesting because the female carries her young, called *joeys*, in her pouch. The *platypus* is a strange mammal that lays eggs like a bird. It also has webbed feet and a bill similar to the duck's. A final example is the *kookaburra*, a bird whose call sounds like a donkey's bray. Hence, its nickname: *laughing jackass*.

What nation is the most crowded?

The tiny European nation of Monaco is probably the most crowded. It has more than 46,000 persons per square mile (17,800 persons per square kilometer). That's about as crowded as the city of Tokyo, Japan.

Is Tokyo the largest city in the world?

No. It ranks third. Shanghai, China, is the largest.

Is Japan a densely populated country?

Yes. It has an average of about 800 persons per square mile (310 persons per square kilometer).

Why is it so crowded?

Simply put, Japan has a large population living in a relatively small area. In number, its population is more than half that of the entire United States, but the Japanese live in an area smaller than the state of Montana.

Isn't Japan an island?

Japan is made up of many islands. It has four main ones and many smaller ones that comprise its territory. There are several nations that consist of island groups.

What are some other island nations?

The Philippines is one. It's made up of more than 7,000 islands off the coast of Southeast Asia. Indonesia, another Southeast Asian nation, has more than 13,600 islands that extend over a distance greater than the distance between Maine and California.

Australia looks like an island, too.

That may be, but it's classified as a continent, not as an island. It's the only country that's also a continent.

Is Australia one of the bigger countries in area?

Yes. Although it's the smallest of the seven continents, it's the sixth largest country in area.

Does Australia have a large population?

Australia has about 14 million persons—fewer than live in the state of New York. Much of Australia's population is made up of immigrants who came to the country from Great Britain and other lands.

Didn't anyone live in Australia before the immigrants?

Yes. Australia's original inhabitants were a unique race of people called Aborigines. There are still about 50,000 full-blooded Aborigines in Australia.

Do Australians speak English?

Yes, though they have an accent different from that of people who live in the United States or Canada.

Do most people in other countries speak English?

No. English is one of the most widely spoken languages. But there are about 3,000 different languages spoken in the world, not counting dialects, which are local forms of languages.

How many languages are spoken in Europe?

There are about 50 different languages and more than 100 dialects spoken in European countries.

Is that more than in any other part of the world?

No. The people of India speak about 180 different languages and more than 700 dialects. In the Indian state of Madhya Pradesh, which is about the size of California, there are more than 375 different languages spoken.

Then how can the Indians communicate?

Communication is a major problem in India. Hindi is the nation's official language, but only about half of all Indians can speak it. Some Indians use English.

Can most of the people in the world read and write?

About 66% of the world's people over age 15 can read and write. But the rate of literacy varies widely from one country to another. In most European countries, a large majority of the people can read and write. But in some countries of Africa and Asia, 90% cannot.

What nation has the highest standard of living?

Standards of living are measured in various ways. One commonly used measurement is the *gross national product,* or GNP. A country's GNP is the total value of all the goods and services it produces.

What countries have the highest total GNP?

Russia, Japan, West Germany, and France rank in that

order, after the United States. It has the highest total GNP of all. The countries that lead in per capita GNP, however, are different.

What is per capita GNP?

Per capita means "per person." So, per capita gross national product is GNP divided by the number of people who live in the country. In order, Qatar, Kuwait, Liechtenstein, United Arab Emirates, and the United States lead the world in per capita GNP.

What nations lead the world in manufacturing?

The United States, Russia, West Germany, Japan, and Great Britain are the leading manufacturing nations.

How about farming? What are some of the major crops produced, and where are they grown?

Wheat and cotton are important. Russia grows more of them than any other nation. China ranks first in rice and tobacco. India leads the world in peanuts, sugar cane, and tea.

And livestock? What countries raise the most cattle and sheep?

India raises more cattle than any other nation in the world. First in the number of sheep is Australia. There are more than 10 times as many sheep as people there. Australia has lots of minerals, too.

Do most countries have minerals and other natural resources?

No, some countries have only a few and must rely on imports to provide them with the raw materials they need. Japan, for example, imports almost all its petroleum and iron ore.

I hear the Middle East has most of the world's oil. Is that true?

The Middle East has more than half the world's known oil reserves. Saudi Arabia is the leading producer of oil there.

Saudi Arabia doesn't produce more oil than any other country?

No. Russia ranks first in oil production.

Does Russia have many other resources?

Yes. Russia's vast territory contains many mineral resources. It has about one-fourth of the world's coal and ranks first in coal production. It also ranks first among all nations in the production of iron ore and manganese.

You haven't mentioned shipping. What country has the biggest shipping industry?

Japan ranks first in shipbuilding. It also has more fishing vessels than any other nation. But Japan is second to Liberia in number of registered merchant ships.

What is the busiest port in the world?

By tonnage, Ras Tanura in Saudi Arabia is the leading port.

1	/
10	∩
100	ϱ
1,000	⌇
10,000	∕
100,000	⌔

is 1,326

Did the Egyptians use hieroglyphics as symbols for their numbers as well as for the objects in their world?

About 3000 BC, the ancient Egyptians used hieroglyphics to write numerals, putting the basic symbols together according to a system based on 10. But the system did not include a zero symbol, nor did it use the principle of place value.

What about railroads? What nation has the most railroad track?

The United States, followed by Russia. But Russia also has the world's longest rail line, which operates between Moscow and Vladivostok. The distance is about 5,600 miles (9,000 kilometers).

There are so many different nations in the world. Are their governments much alike?

No. The forms of government vary among nations. In Western Europe, most have freely elected governments with two or more political parties. Military governments rule many nations elsewhere, and single political parties govern some countries.

What are some nations that have a king or a queen?

Monarchies? Well, Belgium, Denmark, Jordan, Morocco, The Netherlands, and Great Britain are examples of *constitutional monarchies*. But the power of the kings and queens of the world varies. There are some countries with monarchs that hold little power; the parliament, or legislature, actually makes the laws.

How long has Great Britain been a monarchy?

The English monarchy is one of the oldest in the world. It dates back to the AD 800s. The nation we know as Great Britain, however, did not come into being until 1707.

Does Britain have one of the oldest legislatures, too?

Yes. But the oldest legislature of all is the parliament of Iceland, founded in AD 930.

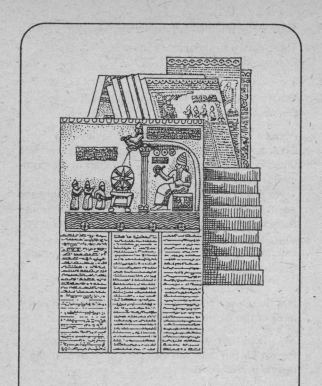

Where were the first libraries?

The first libraries appeared in Mesopotamia, where people discovered that they could produce long-lasting records by making marks on wet clay. Then they dried or baked the clay as tablets. Once their important information had been set down this way, the people established libraries where the clay tablets could be organized.

How many nations have Communist governments?

There are 16 Communist nations. The largest are China and Russia.

What portion of the world's population lives in Communist nations?

About a third of the world's population lives in Communist countries. But not all the people who live under communism are actually members of the Communist party.

For example, only about 6% of Russia's people and about 3% of China's are members of the Communist party in their countries. This is because the membership requirements are strict. The party is also highly centralized: only the top leaders make the important decisions.

Has there ever been one nation that has controlled most of the world's people?

No. There have been many empires in the history of the world. But none has ever controlled most of the people in the world.

What was the biggest empire in history?

The biggest empire in history was the British Empire, which peaked during Queen Victoria's reign in the 1800s.

How big was the British Empire?

At its largest, it covered about a fourth of the world's land and had about a fourth of the world's people. It included many parts of Asia and Africa, as well as Australia, Canada, and New Zealand.

Does Britain still have an empire?

No. During the 1900s, Britain granted independence to almost all its colonies and other dependencies.

So Britain has lost much of its territory, hasn't it?

Yes, and so have many other nations that once founded empires or had advanced civilizations.

What are some examples?

In Africa, Egypt is one of the more notable examples. The pyramids, built more than 4,000 years ago, stand as evidence of Egypt's glory as one of the most powerful civilizations of ancient times. Other early empires centered in what are now India and Iran. And China made many advances in arts, sciences, and technology more than 2,000 years ago.

Ancient Greece was the site of the first advanced European civilization. Later, the Romans controlled a vast empire that extended their influence to many parts of Europe, Africa, and the Middle East.

The Mayan Indians developed the first great civilization in the entire Western Hemisphere in what are now the countries of Belize, El Salvador, Guatemala, Honduras, and Mexico. It flourished from the AD 200s to the 800s.

What happened to these early civilizations?

They eventually declined, and other peoples invaded and conquered them. The conquerors, in turn, established new kingdoms and empires. Over the course of thousands of years, boundaries changed many times. Sometimes they changed because of wars over territory. In other cases people discovered new places and migrated there. The process continues today.

Famous people— a glimpse

How does someone become famous?

There's no rule for becoming famous. There are some who achieve fame because they save lives. An example is Jonas Salk (1914–   ), the doctor known for his work in developing a vaccine against poliomyelitis, or polio, as we commonly call this crippling disease. And there are others like Alexander Graham Bell (1847–1922) who became famous for making life easier. Bell was the American scientist and educator who invented the telephone. Also, don't forget the people who become famous for making life happier. Phineas T. Barnum (1810–91) is one of these. Perhaps the greatest American showman, he created the modern circus.

The U.S. Founding Fathers are famous, aren't they?

Many are. A good example is Thomas Jefferson (1743–1826). The third President of the United States, Jefferson was one of the more talented persons ever to occupy the White House. He was a political philosopher, a writer, an inventor, an educational reformer, an architect, a scientist, and a statesman. He wished, however, to be remembered chiefly as the founder of the University of Virginia and the author of both the Declaration of Independence and the statute of Virginia for religious freedom.

Working for freedom throughout his life, Jefferson was a famous American who worked to enhance, or better, life politically and socially.

Is Benjamin Franklin famous because he worked for freedom?

Benjamin Franklin (1706–90) is famous on many counts. He is one of the earlier illustrious names in U.S. history. Franklin signed four crucial documents during the nation's birth: the Declaration of Independence, the Treaty of Alliance with France, the Treaty of Peace with Great Britain, and U.S. Constitution.

Franklin was a jack-of-all-trades and a master of many. During his long and useful life, he concerned himself not only with matters of state but also with book printing, science, agriculture, and the study of history. Franklin showed the world that lightning is actually electricity, and Franklin's lightning rod saved many buildings from fires caused by lightning. He also invented bifocal lenses, for both distance and reading use. The Franklin Stove, another of his inventions, gave more heat than other stoves of the time and used much less fuel.

One thing Franklin did not do, however, was to become President of the United States.

Who are some outstanding Presidents?

We've already mentioned one: Jefferson. There are many others: George Washington (1732–99) and Abraham Lincoln (1809–65) are two of the best known and perhaps best loved. Another who comes to mind is Franklin Delano Roosevelt (1882–1945). One reason Roosevelt was successful in politics was that millions hailed him as the friend and protector of the common man. Roosevelt led the United States during most of the Great Depression and much of World War II.

There is one thing that sets Roosevelt apart from the other Presidents. He served longer than any other, from 1933 to 1945. Roosevelt was elected President four times, but he did not live to complete his fourth term.

Who was a famous American who never became President?

From recent history, there is Martin Luther King, Jr. (1929–68), winner of the Nobel peace prize in 1964. This great black leader is renowned for his efforts in leading the struggle for black equality through peaceful means. He made constant and stirring pleas for racial equality and justice.

King was famous as a master speaker, and his inspired words provide a poetic legacy for the American people. One example of his way with words is a statement he made when jailed for protesting against injustice and discrimination. King said: "Injustice anywhere is a threat to justice everywhere."

Who is an American woman who fought for social reform?

An early one is Lucy Stone (1818–93), who was the

142

first American woman to lecture on women's rights and women's suffrage, or the right to vote. When Stone and her husband, Henry Blackwell, married, they omitted the word *obey* from their marriage vows. Instead, the couple promised to treat each other equally.

Stone was probably the nation's first married woman to keep her maiden name. She refused to open mail addressed to her as Mrs. Henry Blackwell. One hundred years ago, she created quite a stir.

Who is a famous American woman from recent times?

A U.S. Cabinet member: Patricia Harris (1924–   ). Harris has served as secretary of health, education, and welfare (HEW) and secretary of housing and urban development (HUD). This energetic American earned her law degree at George Washington University in 1960, taught at Howard University School of Law, and later became dean of that school. She was ambassador to Luxembourg and an alternate delegate to the United Nations General Assembly. Besides activity in civil rights and in Democratic party politics, Harris also served as a director of International Business Machines Corporation (IBM).

Who has held the most U.S. Cabinet offices?

Elliot Lee Richardson (1920–   ) has held four different Cabinet offices: secretary of health, education, and welfare (1970–73), secretary of defense (January 1973–May 1973), secretary of commerce (1976 and 1977), and U.S. attorney general (May to October 1973).

Where did Patrick Henry say, "Give me liberty or give me death"?

Patrick Henry spoke these words in 1775 before the Virginia Provincial Convention. Henry, a distinguished statesman and orator at the time of the Revolutionary War, was urging that the Virginia militia be armed for defense of the colony against England. Remembered mainly as a great speaker, Patrick Henry was also an excellent politician and administrator—one of the great U.S. Founding Fathers.

Is it necessary to be a lawyer in order to hold a U.S. Cabinet position?

Not at all. Robert S. McNamara (1916–   ) is an American business leader who was the U.S. secretary of defense from 1961 to 1968. McNamara graduated from the University of California and the Harvard Business School. He became an important adviser to Presidents in economic, foreign, and military matters.

Is it true that some famous American military leaders became Presidents after their military careers ended?

That is correct. They include George Washington, Zachary Taylor (1784–1850), and Ulysses S. Grant (1822–85). A brilliant World War II general who became President is Dwight D. Eisenhower (1890–1969). He became the first Republican President in 20 years, following Franklin Roosevelt and Harry S. Truman (1884–1972). Eisenhower, known as "Ike," campaigned to become President to work for peace. A leader in war, he worked through major challenges with courage and a firm desire to achieve peace. Even Ike's critics never questioned his sincerity.

Are any First Ladies of the United States famous for working for peace or some other humanitarian goal?

Eleanor Roosevelt (1884–1962) is, but her public career began before she became First Lady. She entered politics on the behalf of her husband, Franklin Roosevelt, when he was stricken with polio and became crippled. In the forties and later, Eleanor Roosevelt served as a delegate to the United Nations General Assembly. She also worked for and helped to draft the Universal Declaration of Human Rights. She traveled to Europe, Latin America, and other parts of the world and worked with young people and the underprivileged. She also fought for equal rights for minority groups.

Who is an example of a famous woman in a nation other than the United States?

An excellent example is Golda Meir (1898–1978), prime minister of Israel between 1969 and 1974. Meir actually began her life in Russia, coming in 1906 to live in Milwaukee, Wisconsin, in the United States. She did not settle in Palestine until 1921. During her early career, she served as Israel's minister of labor from 1949 to 1956 and as minister of foreign affairs from 1956 to 1966.

Who is another great prime minister?

From England, there is Winston Churchill (1874–1965), a gallant British leader who warned the world about Russia's *iron curtain*. Churchill, who popularized that term, first used it publicly in a post–World War II speech he gave in 1946 in Fulton, Missouri. Churchill had inspired the Western nations in the World War II fight against fascism (1939–45). After the war, he began to warn of the dissension to come between the democratic nations and the Communist ones.

What is *fascism*?

Fascism is a political philosophy that basically glorifies nation and race. It stands for a centralized government by one person who has unlimited power: a dictator. Fascism calls for strict control of a nation's economy and general society, and for putting down opposition to the fascist government through forceful means. When we think of fascism today, we usually think of its best-known leader: Adolf Hitler.

Who was Adolf Hitler?

Adolf Hitler (1889–1945) was the leader of Germany from 1933 until 1945. He directed the Nazis, the German fascist party members, not only in their World War II effort but also in a campaign of mass slaughter. About 6 million Jews perished in Nazi death camps, where gas chambers, firing squads, torture, starvation, and disease killed thousands every day.

Many people look on Hitler as an archvillain of modern times. He is an excellent example of a leader of tainted fame: an infamous leader.

Were there any other famous national leaders who used cruel measures to achieve their aims?

There are many. One of them was Joseph Stalin (1879–1953), a Communist leader and staunch enemy of Hitler. A Russian dictator, Stalin sought to achieve political unity during the 1930s by conducting "purges," where he eliminated his political enemies by trial and execution and by other means. He achieved his unification goal, but at enormous cost in human life. Later, Nikita Khrushchev, Russia's dictator from 1958 to 1964, revealed the truth about Stalin's "Rule by Terror."

For what is Khrushchev well known?

Khrushchev is well known for trying to raise living standards in Russia. But in this effort he did not do so well as hoped. He was however successful in greatly changing foreign policy in post-Stalin Russia. Khrushchev believed in peaceful coexistence with Western nations and redirected Russia's foreign policies along those lines.

Was Napoleon Bonaparte born in France?

No, Napoleon Bonaparte was not born in France, even though he is one of France's famous leaders. And this military genius did not come from a French family. He was the son of an Italian nobleman and was born in Corsica, an island owned by France. He didn't begin to learn French until he was about ten. His early military ambition wasn't to conquer Europe for France, but to free Corsica from French domination.

Is there a great twentieth-century Communist leader from a country other than Russia?

In China, Mao Tse-Tung (1893–1976) helped to make communism an important force in modern times. He led the long struggle that made China a Communist nation in 1949. Mao's round face with a mole on the chin became familiar throughout the world. His writings, particularly those on guerrilla warfare and the role of peasants in Communist revolutions, are influential outside China.

Aren't there any national leaders who found nonviolent methods to achieve their goals?

There certainly are. Mohandas K. Gandhi (1869–1948) fought nonviolently for the freedom of India from Great Britain. Gandhi's limitless physical and moral strength helped to free India from British control by a unique method of nonviolent resistance. He believed that we can know truth only through tolerance and concern for our fellows. Gandhi developed a method of direct social action based upon principles of courage, nonviolence, and truth. He called this nonviolent method *satyagraha*. Altogether, Gandhi spent seven years in prison for nonviolent resistance to the domination of Great Britain. India gained its independence finally in 1947, a year before Gandhi's death.

Who was one of the greatest scientists of all time?

Albert Einstein (1879–1955) goes down in history as one of the greatest. He is best known for his theory of relativity, which revolutionized scientific thought. Although Einstein was not associated with any orthodox religion, this genius' nature was deeply religious. Merely being around him was a profoundly spiritual experience for those fortunate enough to know him. It was Einstein's research that laid the base for controlling the release of energy from the atom. His famous equation $E = mc^2$ (energy equals mass times the velocity of light squared) became one cornerstone in the development of atomic energy.

What of the famous explorers? What do we know about them?

We know that they were persons of enormous daring and energy. Think of Christopher Columbus (1451–1506), the determined explorer who left on the famous voyage that led him to the shores of America. Columbus set sail with three ships. The largest, the *Santa Maria*, was probably only 75 to 90 feet (23 to 27 meters) long. It carried a crew of only 40 persons and took 36 days—over five weeks—to cross the Atlantic. Compare that to some modern ocean liners, which are about 1,000 feet (300 meters) long and can carry about 3,000 persons. Some liners cross the Atlantic in less than 5 days.

Are the space explorers like the explorers of the earth?

Probably in some ways. People of daring seem to be born to every generation. All explorers probably have that trait to some degree. John Glenn (1921–   ) is a modern explorer, the first American to orbit the earth (1962). Today, Glenn is a U.S. Senator from Ohio.

Glenn exhibits one characteristic present in some great achievers: a modest approach to his accomplishment. When talking about his orbit, he always uses "*we*" instead of "*I*." He never forgets that it took thousands of persons to send him safely into space and bring him back again.

What was the next great accomplishment in the exploration of space?

The exploration of space involves a long chain of successes, one leading to another. But one of the great accomplishments after Glenn's orbit occurred when an astronaut actually "walked" in space. The American who did this in 1966 was Edwin E. Aldrin, Jr. (1930–   ), the pilot of the Gemini 12 space flight.

Why was walking in space important to the space effort?

It was important because the successful effort proved that people can work outside an orbiting space vehicle.

One of the next steps in the chain was walking on the moon, wasn't it?

Yes, and the American who was the first person to set foot on the moon was astronaut Neil A. Armstrong (1930–   ). He and Aldrin, the first space "walker," landed the Apollo 11 lunar module on the moon on July 20, 1969.

Shortly after landing, Armstrong stepped out on the surface of the moon and said: "That's one small step for a man; one giant leap for mankind." Armstrong's message was directed toward his fellows on earth as he accomplished his great feat. It was an appropriate message at so historical a moment; for the famous persons throughout civilization have exercised a great influence—sometimes good, sometimes harmful—on the average life.

Art and the artist

What are some of the older art forms?

Several art forms date back to prehistoric times. Music
and dance are probably among the oldest, though no
one knows exactly when they first developed. As long
ago as 35,000 BC, people carved designs into bone.
By about 20,000 BC, prehistoric artists modeled in
clay and painted on rock.

What do prehistoric clay sculptures look like?

Most prehistoric sculptures are animals and figures of
plump women. The female figures may have repre-
sented goddesses or women bearing children.

Were these sculptures used as decorations?

Probably not. Prehistoric people may have believed that the sculptures had magical and religious qualities. They probably used the sculptures in rituals dealing with topics like death and fertility.

What are the main subjects of prehistoric paintings?

Animals and hunters are the main subjects.

Where have prehistoric paintings been found?

Some of the finest examples are on the walls of caves in the border regions of France and Spain.

What did prehistoric artists use as paints?

They rubbed naturally colored materials into animal fats to produce a pastelike paint. They made black paint from charcoal and manganese oil, white paint from clay and lime mud, and red and yellow paints from animal blood and iron compounds.

What kinds of materials do painters use today?

Some of the colored pigments that painters use today still come from natural earth materials. Other pigments are made artificially. Different kinds of paints are made by mixing pigments with one of a number of different substances called binders. These include vegetable oil, water, beeswax, egg yolk, certain kinds of glue, and synthetic resin.

Is there a painter considered the greatest of all time?

Many painters have achieved lasting fame at various times for various reasons. But most critics would agree that Leonardo da Vinci ranks as one of the greatest painters of all times. His *Mona Lisa* is probably the most famous painting in the world.

When did da Vinci paint the *Mona Lisa*?

He completed the work in about 1503 during the Renaissance, a period when painting, sculpture, architecture, literature, and other arts flourished.

Did the Renaissance last for a long time?

It lasted for about 300 years. The Renaissance began in Italy around 1300. Then it spread throughout Europe during the 1400s and 1500s.

Who were some other famous Renaissance artists?

The famous Italian Renaissance artists included Giotto, Donatello, Sandro Botticelli, and Raphael. Flemish painters were Jan van Eyck and Pieter Bruegel the Elder. In Spain, there was the master El Greco. One of the most versatile and talented of all Renaissance artists was Michelangelo. He created outstanding works in three art fields: painting, sculpture, and architecture.

What are Michelangelo's more famous works?

Michelangelo's most famous painting is probably the series of Biblical scenes he painted on the ceiling of the Sistine Chapel in the Vatican in Rome. He worked on the ceiling from 1508 to 1512.

Michelangelo's best-known sculptures include his huge statue of David, and the *Pietà*, which portrays the Virgin Mary and the dead figure of Jesus. Michelangelo sculpted the *Pietà* when he was only 23 years old.

When was the first commercial showing of motion pictures in the United States?

The first commercial showing of motion pictures in the United States took place in 1896. Then, the *nickelodeon*—the first movie theater—appeared. Nickelodeons were stores converted into theaters by adding chairs. Admission was five cents. These theaters showed silent movies while a pianist played music that fit the action on the screen. Audiences consisted mainly of laborers, many of them immigrants.

What is an example of Michelangelo's architecture?

Michelangelo's outstanding contribution to architecture was his design for the dome of St. Peter's Church in Rome. It became a model for many other domes.

Is architecture an old art?

Yes, it is an ancient art. One of the first architects was Imhotep, an Egyptian who designed the first-known pyramid more than 4,500 years ago. The pyramids are considered a wonder of ancient architecture.

How big are the pyramids?

They vary in size. But the largest of all, the Great Pyramid, has a base large enough to hold 10 football fields. Its original height was 481 feet (147 meters). The Great Pyramid still stands on the west bank of the Nile, just outside Cairo.

What does the inside of a pyramid look like?

Inside there are long, narrow corridors that lead to one or more burial chambers. Sometimes paintings on the chamber walls depict scenes from Egyptian life. Some of the paintings that decorate pyramid walls and the walls of other ancient tombs provide a priceless source of information about the history of other art forms.

Which art forms do the pyramids tell us about?

Well, music and dance, for example. Many ancient Egyptian tomb paintings portray dancers and musicians. By looking at the paintings, historians can tell what sorts of musical instruments people used thousands of years ago.

What were some of the earlier musical instruments?

Many people would say that the human voice was the earliest instrument of all. But the first musical instrument that people constructed was the drum. The ancient Egyptians used various kinds of drums and other percussion instruments, or instruments sounded by striking, shaking, or scraping. The Egyptians also played harps and other string instruments, wind instruments, and trumpets.

Did early musicians play together in orchestras?

Musicians have played together in groups for thousands of years. But what we think of as an orchestra—a group of players with many different instruments—didn't really begin to develop until about 300 years ago.

Who were some of the leading composers of early orchestral music?

Johann Sebastian Bach, Joseph Haydn, and Wolfgang Amadeus Mozart were three of the greatest. Bach came from an extraordinary musical family. From the 1500s through the 1700s, more than 50 members of Bach's family became recognized musicians.

What kinds of music did Haydn write?

Haydn wrote music in various forms including works for voice, for string quartets, and for orchestras. But Haydn is known as the "father of the symphony" because he developed this form of music into a long, complex work for large orchestras. He wrote more than 100 symphonies.

Did Mozart compose symphonies, too?

Yes, and during his short career he composed a tremendous variety of other works, as well. Mozart was born in 1756 and began composing music when he was 5. Although he died before his thirty-sixth birthday, he composed more than 600 musical works including symphonies, church music, violin and piano concertos, and operas.

Who composed the first opera?

In 1597, Jacopo Peri composed *Dafne*, which we generally consider to be the first opera.

When did ballet develop?

Ballet developed about the same time as opera. Italian dancers performed the first ballet at a royal wedding in Paris in 1581. Ballet and opera both developed as ways to add musical elements to Greek myths and other works of ancient literature.

Did literature originate in ancient Greece?

No. Ancient Greece had a tremendous influence on the development of literature. But the origins of literature go back to the origins of the written word. The first people to use a system of word writing were the Sumerians. About 5,000 years ago, they lived in what is now Iraq. The earliest Sumerian literature was produced around the end of the 3000s BC.

What other early peoples produced literature?

Many other groups including Assyrians, Babylonians, Egyptians, Hebrews, Indians, Chinese, and Persians. Some early Oriental literature influenced later Western works. Many of Aesop's fables, for example, came from Oriental tales.

Did the Greeks produce the most outstanding early literature?

No. The Hebrews' Old Testament of the Bible ranks as the outstanding work of early literature. It is also one of the more influential works ever written, forming the basis of religious and moral beliefs of many peoples.

How did the ancient Greeks influence the development of literature?

The ancient Greeks produced epic poems, tragic and comic dramas, histories, philosophical essays, biographies, and other works of literature that are still considered models of form. And artists have used themes from Greek literature countless times in more modern pieces of literature. These include several of the works of William Shakespeare, probably the world's most popular author.

Why is Shakespeare considered the world's most popular author?

Shakespeare's plays have been produced more times and read in more countries than the works of any other playwright. In addition to his ranking as the world's greatest playwright, Shakespeare is considered the finest English-language poet of all time. Through his 37 plays and numerous poems, Shakespeare had a tremendous influence on the development of the English language.

What is the world's largest indoor stadium?

The world's largest indoor stadium is the Louisiana Superdome. It lies at the edge of downtown New Orleans. The 95,427-seat stadium houses conventions, sports events, and trade shows.

How did Shakespeare influence the English language?

Shakespeare used new variations of grammar and even invented new words and phrases. Some are commonly used today.

What are some examples of words and phrases that Shakespeare invented?

Scholars credit Shakespeare with originating the common words *bump, lonely,* and *assassination.* His phrases include *fair play, catch cold, a foregone conclusion,* and *disgraceful conduct.*

Was Shakespeare popular in his own time?

Yes, but his audience has grown tremendously in the more than 300 years since his death. One modern art form, the motion picture, has enabled millions of persons to see Shakespeare's plays performed.

Were plays the subjects of the first movies?

No. Plays tell stories. The first motion pictures did not.

If they didn't tell stories, what did the first movies do?

The first movies simply showed various moving things: a train pulling into a station, a parade, and a waterfall, for example.

When was the first movie made?

No one knows exactly when the first movie was made. But during the 1880s, various inventors worked on ways to make and project movies. Motion pictures were first projected on a screen publicly in 1895 in Paris.

When did movies first appear in the United States?

In 1896, Thomas Edison presented the first U.S. public screening of a motion picture.

What was Edison's movie about?

The movie included scenes of a boxing match, waves on a beach, and a dance performance.

When did movies begin to tell stories?

The movies began to tell stories around 1899, when a French magician named Georges Méliès began filming fairy tales and science fiction stories.

Were the first American movies made in Hollywood?

No. Most of the earliest movies were made in New York City and in Fort Lee, New Jersey.

How did Hollywood become a center for movie production?

Movie producers realized that the climate and the variety of natural scenery around Los Angeles made the area ideal for making movies. In 1911, the first motion picture studio was built in the district of Los Angeles called Hollywood. Many other studios followed.

When did movies first use sound?

Some of the earlier movies used phonograph recordings or piano music to add sound to the filmed action. But sound wasn't part of a film until 1927, when Al Jolson spoke a few lines in the movie *The Jazz Singer*.

Did movies become more popular after the introduction of sound?

Absolutely. Movie attendance soared during the late 1920s. And movies continued to be one of the more popular forms of American entertainment until the development of television in the late 1940s.

Did television affect movie attendance?

Yes. In the late 1940s, there were about 90 million weekly moviegoers in the United States. The number dropped to fewer than 20 million in the mid-1970s. Television also ended the golden age of radio. From about 1925 to 1950, radio had provided many Americans with a major source of entertainment.

Do most American homes today have television?

About 96% of all American homes have television. There are more television sets per person in the United States than in any other country in the world.

Then television makes entertainment available to almost everyone in the United States, doesn't it?

Yes. Television serves various purposes, but it is probably unrivaled as a convenient source of entertainment. Through television, countless millions can enjoy drama, music, dance—and virtually all the other performing arts.

Attention: Sports!

What do people talk about more than the weather?

Some people say sports. No one has measured how much, but it's a safe bet to say that sports occupy a lot of human time and interest.

Sports are a common meeting ground for people from all parts of the world. There are, for instance, the Olympic Games. Athletes from many nations come to these to compete in all kinds of sports events. Also, there are the Pan American Games, sponsored by 29 Western Hemisphere nations. And we have the world championship tournaments for specific games such as the tournament for tennis held each summer in Wimbledon, England.

What's the favorite sport in the United States?

Around World Series time, you'd be sure it was baseball. A philosopher and teacher at Columbia University, Jacques Barzun (1907-   ), said, "Whoever wants to know the heart and mind of America had better learn baseball."

How did baseball develop?

From a game called rounders, which the English played as early as the 1600s. Rounders, like baseball, involved hitting a ball with a bat and advancing around bases. American colonists in New England played rounders as early as the 1700s. They called the game by several names, including *town ball*, the *Massachusetts game*, and, sometimes, *base ball*. Rules for the game appeared in books from time to time. Even so, people generally played the game according to their local customs.

What was the first baseball club?

The first organized baseball team was the Knickerbocker Base Ball Club of New York. It organized in 1845. Its written rules, with those added later, did much to make baseball the game it is today.

What was early major league baseball like?

Well, we call that period the "dead ball era" of baseball. The baseballs used until about 1920 were "dead"; that is, less lively than those used today. Most batters were place hitters rather than long ball hitters. Wee Willie Keeler, a leading batter of baseball's early days, stated the batting philosophy of the era. His famous motto was: "I hit 'em where they ain't."

1816

1866

How long have people had bikes to ride?

People have had bikes only since around 1790.
But pedals were not added to the invention
until 1839. Until then riders would walk and
glide, walk and glide.

What are the baseball pitches today?

The most common are the fast ball, the curve ball, and the slider. A fast ball thrown by a major league pitcher may travel at a speed close to 100 miles (160 kilometers) per hour. A curve ball thrown by a right-handed pitcher breaks sharply to the left and downward as it reaches the batter. A left-hander's curve breaks to the right and downward. A slider resembles a curve ball. But it seems to "slide" rather than break sharply, and it does not move downward.

How are the players chosen for an all-star baseball game?

The baseball fans choose the starting lineups—except for the pitchers—for the two teams in an all-star game. This game, of course, matches outstanding American League players against stars of the National League. The team managers select the starting pitchers and all substitutes.

Who broke Babe Ruth's career record for home runs?

Outfielder Henry Aaron of the Milwaukee (now Atlanta) Braves did. Babe Ruth had hit a record 714 homers when he retired in 1935. Henry Aaron batted his 715th homer in 1974 and his 755th by the time he retired after the 1976 season.

There's nothing more exciting than a home run, is there?

Not unless it's a perfect pass to the end zone for a touchdown.

When did forward passing begin in football?

The first forward pass was thrown for an 18-yard gain by Wesleyan University against Yale in 1906. But passing did not become popular until 1913 in a game between Notre Dame and Army. The Army team was favored to win because it was stronger and heavier than Notre Dame. But Gus Dorais, the Notre Dame quarterback, threw the ball several times to Knute Rockne, a star end, and Notre Dame won, 35 to 13. From then on, forward passing made football more popular than ever. It let smaller, faster players compete successfully in the game. It also required careful planning and the use of many different plays.

When was college football organized?

Organized college football began in 1876. That year, Harvard, Yale, Princeton, and Columbia formed the American Intercollegiate Football Association, the first college football conference. Today, most of the more than 600 college and university football teams belong to one of about 60 college conferences. These conferences set standards for competition and are made up of teams of about the same strength.

How about professional football?

The town teams of the late 1800s became the first professional football teams when they began paying college players to play for them. Each player in the first professional game in 1895 in Latrobe, Pennsylvania, received $10. Soon, with increased competition between town teams, especially in the Midwest, college football players were being paid as much as $600 a game.

Since 1920, with the founding of the American Professional Football Association, there have been many football associations and leagues that have organized this kind of football. During the 1950s, professional football gained great popularity. Television networks began paying millions of dollars for the rights to televise games. Teams of various leagues offered some college stars as much as $500,000 salary and bonus over a period of several years to play for them.

When was the first bowl game?

The first bowl game was the Rose Bowl in 1902, when Michigan defeated Stanford, 49 to 0. Then the Sugar Bowl began in 1935 in New Orleans.

Speaking of "bowl" games, how did the sport of bowling begin?

Bowling is one of the older and more popular indoor sports. Every year in the United States, about 39 million persons roll balls down gleaming wooden lanes to try to knock down the 10 pins facing today's bowlers. U.S. players originally used 9, not 10, pins.

Why did U.S. bowlers change from 9 to 10 pins?

In 1841, the Connecticut legislature outlawed "bowling at nine pins" because gambling on the sport had become widespread. Bowlers evaded the ban by adding a pin; thus started the 10-pin game. Now, there are huge bowling establishments. The largest one in the world opened in Tokyo in 1970. It has 504 lanes.

That's more lanes than there are miles in the Indianapolis Motor Speedway!

That's true. The automobile racers at the Indianapolis

Motor Speedway face a 500-mile course. The Indy 500, the most famous race on the Championship Trail, goes for 200 laps around the paved oval Indianapolis Motor Speedway. The 1978 winner, Al Unser, traveled at 161.36 miles per hour (295.68 kilometers per hour).

Who holds the record as the world's fastest automobile driver?

That is Gary Gabelich. In 1970, he drove his rocket-powered car, the Blue Flame, 622.4 miles per hour (1001.7 kilometers per hour) on Utah's Bonneville Salt Flats.

Which U.S. sport attracts more people than any other?

Horse racing. Racing fans thrill to the sight of colorfully dressed jockeys on sleek horses galloping around a track toward the finish line.

How does a jockey help his horse during a race?

The jockey can determine a horse's success by techniques of riding and guiding the horse. There are two basic riding positions. American jockeys use the crouch position for riding, in which the rider leans forward over the horse's neck. European jockeys sit upright. All jockeys must be lightweight, about 110 pounds (50 kilograms).

Who is a famous jockey?

Steve Cauthen is one. In 1977, as a 17-year-old apprentice jockey, Cauthen rode 488 winners and won $6,151,750 in purses.

What's another sport involving horses?

Polo. In 1862, a group of British officers copied the game from tribal horsemen in Punjab, India.

Do polo horses have special characteristics?

They must have strong nervous systems. It takes six months to a year to train a polo pony. The horse must become used to having clubs swung near its head. It must also be able to stop quickly, turn, twist, and resume stride with little loss of speed. Most difficult of all, upon the command of its rider the horse must have the courage to bump into another horse at angles up to 45 degrees.

Isn't the equipment for polo somewhat the same as for ice hockey?

The players in both games use sticks to drive the ball or puck through the goal. Polo, of course, is played on horses, while hockey is played on ice skates. The teams for both games are rather small—four for polo and six for hockey—and the rules of the games resemble each other. In both sports, two opposing teams try to drive the ball or puck through their opponents' goal.

How fast can a hockey puck travel?

Faster than 100 miles per hour (160 kilometers per hour). A goalkeeper on each team defends the team's net. Goalkeepers must often make lightning slides across the front of the net on their knees, stomach, or back to block shots of the puck. The fast, rough action of hockey is testified to by the fact that there's a rule that allows substitution of players while play is in progress.

What are the skills ice hockey players must have?

There are five: *Skating* is the most important. A player must be able to turn sharply, skate backwards, and perform many other maneuvers—all at top speed. *Stick-handling* moves the puck first with one side of the hockey stick's blade and then with the other while the player is skating. Some sweeps of the stick are wide and some narrow to keep the opponent guessing. *Passing* the puck to a teammate involves three different maneuvers: flat passes across the ice; flip passes up and over the ice; and drop passes, or simply leaving the puck behind where a teammate can get it. *Shooting,* the fourth required skill for hockey, is the one needed to drive the puck into the net and so score goals. Finally, in *checking,* a player can use his stick to hook or poke the puck away from an opponent's stick. Or he can bump against an opponent with his hip or shoulder to try to block his progress or throw him off balance.

Is there a fairly new team sport?

Basketball is fairly recent. We can trace this sport to 1891. James A. Naismith invented basketball at the International YMCA Training School in Springfield, Massachusetts, in 1891. Naismith was asked to create a team sport that could be played indoors during the winter, so he formed 13 basic rules for the game. Then he asked a janitor to nail two boxes to the gymnasium balcony for use as goals. But the janitor could find only some half-bushel baskets, which Naismith accepted. The sport thus became known as *basket*ball. The game spread quickly to high schools, colleges, and semiprofessional and professional teams throughout the United States and Canada. During the 1970s, because of the national televising of major games, basketball became even more popular.

Where was the first baseball game held?

The first game of organized baseball took place at Hoboken in 1846. The New York Nine defeated the New York Knickerbockers 23 to 1.

Has basketball always been as fast paced as it is today?

No, the fast-paced style of play developed from 1935 to 1938, when Angelo (Hank) Luisetti of Stanford University set many scoring records with a new kind of shot: a long, one-handed push shot. Before then, most players scored by shooting from under the basket or by shooting a two-handed shot with both feet set firmly on the floor. Today's play is much faster.

Speed is important in swimming, too, isn't it?

It can be. Modern swimmers have a great variety of fast and slower water sports to choose from: diving, surfing, water-skiing, water polo, scuba diving, and synchronized swimming are examples. Water sports also include fishing and boating.

When did swimming become a major competitive sport?

During the 1900s. Today, thousands of swimmers compete in meets held by schools, colleges, and swimming clubs. The best international swimmers take part in annual meets in many parts of the world. Swimming races have always been a highlight of the Summer Olympic Games.

Who are swimmers who hold speed records?

For men, Rod Strachan of the United States holds the world swimming record for the 400-meter individual medley (1 meter = 1.1 yards). He set the record at Montreal in July 1976 at the Olympic games. The time was 4 minutes, 23.68 seconds. For women, the winner that year in the 400-meter was Ulrike Tauber of East Germany with 4 minutes, 42.77 seconds.

What underwater sports are there?

Skin diving and scuba diving. There are strange and lovely sights beneath the surface of rivers, lakes, and oceans. These sports make them available to the swimmer.

What's the equipment needed for diving?

Most skin divers wear a face mask, swim fins, and they use a short breathing tube called a snorkel. Scuba diving involves the use of portable metal tanks of compressed air from which the diver breathes. The name scuba stands for self-contained underwater breathing apparatus. The equipment consists of one or more tanks strapped to the diver's back, plus an air hose and a demand regulator, which controls the air to the diver's lungs. Also needed are a face mask, a wet suit, a weighted belt, swim fins, a snorkel, and a flotation vest.

How far can divers go underwater?

Most breath-hold divers can descend 30 to 40 feet (9 to 12 meters) and must surface after less than a minute. There are some divers, however, who can dive as far as 100 feet (30 meters) and remain submerged for about two minutes. A scuba diver using one tank can stay at a depth of 40 feet (12 meters) for about an hour. Strenuous activity or increased depth, however, uses up a diver's air supply more rapidly.

What's another water sport?

Water-skiing. And it's convenient. Water-skiing equipment can be rented at most waterside resorts. The water skier holds on to a tow rope attached to a motorboat and is pulled across the surface of the water. Outboard boats of 25 horsepower (19 kilowatts) or more, and inboard boats of 50 horsepower (37 kilowatts) or over, are the kinds most often used for water-skiing.

Is the same kind of skis used for water-skiing and snow skiing?

No. They resemble each other, but water skis are wider than snow skis.

Is snow skiing a modern sport?

It began about 1850, when a Norwegian named Sondre Norheim invented the first stiff bindings, the straps that keep the skis on the foot. Norheim made his bindings by tying twisted pieces of wet birch roots around his boots. As the roots dried, they became stiff. The bindings held the skis more securely than leather straps and so provided the control needed to make turns. Other techniques developed out of this, and by 1900 skiing became a sport. It was introduced into the Olympic Games in 1924.

What would you see if you attended the opening of the Olympic Games?

Thousands of spectators are seated in the stadium. The athletes from the various countries march in. The Olympic flag goes up, trumpets play, and cannon boom in salute. Then into the air fly hundreds of doves: a symbol of peace. With torches, the members of the Greek team run in and light the Olympic flame; and the games begin.

Index